P9-BZW-288

Also by Patrick Lencioni

The Five Temptations of a CEO

The Four Obsessions of an Extraordinary Executive

The Five Dysfunctions of a Team

Death by Meeting

Overcoming the Five Dysfunctions of a Team

The Truth About Employee Engagement

The Three Big Questions for a Frantic Family

Getting Naked

The Advantage

The Ideal Team Player

Silos, Politics, and Turf Wars

A LEADERSHIP FABLE
ABOUT DESTROYING THE
BARRIERS THAT TURN
COLLEAGUES INTO COMPETITORS

Patrick Lencioni

Published by Jossey-Bass
A Wiley Imprint
One Montgomery, Ste. 1200, San Francisco, CA 94104 www.josseybass.com

Jossey-Bass books and products are available through most bookstores. To contact Jossey-Bass directly call our Customer Care Department within the U.S. at 800-956-7739, outside the U.S. at 317-572-3986, or fax 317-572-4002.

Jossey-Bass also publishes its books in a variety of electronic formats. Some content that appears in print may not be available in electronic books.

Library of Congress Cataloging-in-Publication Data

Lencioni, Patrick, 1965-
Silos, politics, and turf wars : a leadership fable about destroying the barriers that turn colleagues into competitors / Patrick Lencioni.
p. cm.
ISBN-13: 978-0-7879-7638-5 (cloth)
ISBN-10: 0-7879-7638-5 (cloth)
1. Leadership. 2. Organizational behavior. I. Title: Silos, politics and turf wars. II. Title.
HD57.7.L449 2006
658.4'092-dc22

2005033968

Printed in the United States of America
FIRST EDITION
HB Printing V008524_122818

CONTENTS

Introduction vii

The Fable

Part One: Entrepreneurial Ambition 3
Part Two: Roller Coaster 19
Part Three: Rally 77
Part Four: Moments of Truth 139

The Theory

Introduction to Silos 175
Components of the Model 178
Identifying a Thematic Goal 187
Case Studies 189
Managing and Organizing Around the Thematic Goal 197
Thematic Goals and Long-Term Context 202
Making Matrix Organizations Work 205
Getting Started 207

Acknowledgments 209

About the Author 211

This book is dedicated to my dear friends at The Table Group: Amy, Tracy, Karen, Michele, and Jeff. Your dedication and talent amaze me more every day and cannot be put into words adequately.

INTRODUCTION

Silos. It's a word I first started hearing in a corporate context more than twenty years ago, always used to describe departmental politics and territoriality within organizations. At the time, I thought it was one of those terms that would eventually go away like so much other management jargon—but it hasn't.

In fact, today the word seems to provoke the same level of frustration that it did back then, if not more. When I told some of my clients that I was planning to write a book about silos, they seemed to have a universally visceral reaction: "Pleeease write that book. The silos in this company are driving me crazy!"

Which would seem to be a good thing—proposing a solution to a problem that people are hungry to solve—except that my view of silos might not be what some leaders expect to hear.

That's because many executives I've worked with who struggle with silos are inclined to look down into their organizations and wonder, "Why don't those employees just learn to get along better with people in other departments? Don't they know we're all on the same team?" All too often this sets off a well-intentioned but ill-advised series of actions—training programs, memos, posters—designed to inspire people to work better together.

But these initiatives only provoke cynicism among employees—who would love nothing more than to eliminate the turf wars and departmental politics that often make their work lives miserable. The problem is, they can't do anything about it. Not without help from their leaders.

And while the first step those leaders need to take is to address any behavioral problems that might be preventing executive team members from working well with one another—that was the thrust of my book *The Five Dysfunctions of a Team*—even behaviorally cohesive teams can struggle with silos. (Which is particularly frustrating and tragic because it leads well-intentioned and otherwise functional team members to inappropriately question one another's trust and commitment to the team.)

To tear down silos, leaders must go beyond behaviors and address the contextual issues at the heart of departmental separation and politics. The purpose of this book is to present a simple, powerful tool for addressing those issues and reducing the pain that silos cause. And that pain should not be underestimated.

Silos—and the turf wars they enable—devastate organizations. They waste resources, kill productivity, and jeopardize the achievement of goals.

But beyond all that, they exact a considerable human toll too. They cause frustration, stress, and disillusionment by forcing employees to fight bloody, unwinnable battles with people who should be their teammates. There is perhaps no greater cause of professional anxiety and exasperation—not to mention turnover—than employees having to fight with people in their own organization. Understandably and inevitably, this bleeds over into their personal lives, affecting family and friends in profound ways.

The good news is that this is all immensely avoidable. In fact, I have never used a tool with clients that has been so universally and successfully adopted.

Like my other books, *Silos, Politics, and Turf Wars* is written in the form of a realistic but fictional story. Unlike those books, however, it involves not one but a host of different companies struggling to eliminate infighting from their organizations and bring about a sense of alignment and sanity.

I sincerely hope that this book helps you do the same.

The Fable

PART ONE

Entrepreneurial Ambition

HONEYMOON

Five months. That's how long it took for Jude Cousins' entrepreneurial passion and excitement to fade into anxiety and panic. While it was true that he had never started a company before and didn't know exactly what to expect, five months just seemed like too short of a honeymoon to Jude.

To be fair, Cousins Consulting wasn't really a company. Just a consulting practice operating out of a spare bedroom in Jude's home. No employees. No politics. Just Jude, his passion, and three clients. Two of which, unfortunately, were already in jeopardy.

HATCH

For the seven years prior to starting his consulting firm, Jude had received nothing but encouragement and recognition in his career, which only served to magnify his frustration as an entrepreneur.

After a brief and unsatisfying postcollege stint in journalism, Jude took a job in the marketing department at Hatch Technology, a fast-growing company that developed financial software for consumers and small businesses. Beginning his career at Hatch as a copy editor, Jude gradually worked his way through every department in the marketing division, with detours into product management and operations.

As a result of his work ethic, humility, and general curiosity about whatever he was doing—not to mention the rapid growth of the company—promotions came frequently for Jude. At the age of twenty-eight, four years after joining Hatch, he was named director of corporate communication, reporting directly to the company's vice president of marketing.

Jude's career trajectory, though impressive on its own merit, was all the more amazing given his relative lack of passion for technology. Not particularly inspired by the charter of enticing people to buy software, he knew that the secret to his success had everything to do with his insatiable passion for learning. As Jude liked to tell his friends, he felt like he was being paid to go to business school.

And being just one level removed from the senior executive team meant Jude was constantly exposed to challenges related to every aspect of running a company, from strategy to structure to management. All of which fascinated him.

Still, he was not content to have his education limited to one company. So Jude began volunteering to sit on a variety of advisory boards for small but growing companies in the area, all of whom were happy to have someone of his talent providing advice, especially when that advice was free of charge.

Jude was eagerly soaking up everything he could—and forming strong opinions about how he would run a company, which he had come to believe was the ultimate goal of his professional life. Anyone who knew Jude assumed he would one day be a CEO.

SMOOTH SAILING

On a personal level, Jude's life certainly seemed to be heading in the right direction.

He and his wife of three years, Theresa, were hoping to start a family as soon as possible. They had recently bought their first home, a small but attractive rancher in Orinda, just over the hills from the San Francisco Bay. Though not wealthy, they were financially more secure than ever, and more important, had amassed a close-knit collection of friends in the area. They were involved in their local church, and were quick to help friends, neighbors, and family members who needed a hand.

From a day-to-day professional standpoint, Jude had everything he needed. Between his responsibilities at Hatch and the variety of companies he was being exposed to as an adviser, he had no complaints. His work was interesting enough, and his workload, though substantial, was manageable. Jude certainly had no intention of changing his career.

Until the merger.

BATCH

Though it had been announced to the press as a "merger of equals," anyone with a sense of the market knew that Hatch Technology was on the losing end of the acquisition by its slightly larger competitor, Bell Financial Systems. Carter Bell, the company's brash CEO, had a much higher profile in the industry and wasn't about to lose control of his corporation in a merger.

But because he didn't want to rock the new boat too soon after the deal was closed, he chose to build something of a Noah's Ark management team: two heads of sales, two heads of marketing, and so on. As a result, the seeds of discontent were planted within the new organization, which would cleverly be called "Batch Systems." Employees would later joke that the name combination should have been reversed and called—*Hell.*

Fortunately, market analysts seemed to like the merger more than Batch employees did. So Jude and his colleagues gladly watched the stock price rise with every painful passing week after the merger papers had been signed.

As for Jude, his duties and title were divvied up between him and his counterpart from Bell, so he took on a slightly diminished role as director of advertising. After overcoming his initial disappointment in the change in title and responsibility, Jude accepted his new situation. In fact, he began to like the arrangement, which gave him more time for his wife, his golf, and his advisory boards.

Maybe this is just what the doctor ordered, Jude tried to convince himself.

POLITICS

With every week that passed, Jude found it harder and harder to get things done. Meetings were longer and more frequent than ever, and required increasingly more political dexterity. Back-channel deal making seemed to be taking over as the primary means of communication and decision making, with finger-pointing running a close second.

Jude was honest enough to admit that Hatch hadn't been a perfect company before the merger; without looking too hard, departmental skirmishes and divisional competition could certainly be found. But since the merger, infighting had risen to a new level entirely. Attention had shifted drastically inward, away from issues like customers and competitors and toward battles over budgets, titles, and responsibility for mistakes.

And while it could be expected that these feuds might develop between employees of the two former companies, new levels of intercompany conflict were rising in other areas too. There was the headquarters versus field office split. And sales versus engineering. And even within marketing, turf wars were as ridiculous as they were damaging.

Perhaps the most unbelievable example occurred more than two months after the merger. The forum for the travesty would be a leading trade publication, *Technology Today*.

Hatch had always maintained a strong advertising presence in the publication, as had Bell. During a meeting of the new marketing departments, Jude proposed a new coordinated approach to advertising, one that would allow Batch to double its overall coverage, but with a more focused, consistent message about the new company's combined product suite.

After a short presentation of the new ad strategy, complete with mockups of the artwork and ads themselves, Jude was relieved to see a roomful of heads nodding and to hear a chorus of "looks good" and "sounds fine to me" from his colleagues.

Two weeks later, *Technology Today* hit newsstands. Pages forty and forty-one contained Jude's ads, highlighting Batch's new suite of products and the discounted prices available for customers who chose to buy them together in bundles.

Unfortunately, page twenty-eight contained an unrelated ad for Bell Technology, with no mention of Batch at all! Not only that, the prices for the old Bell products had actually been reduced to a level below those of the combined set, which would only encourage customers to buy them separately.

Though not prone to anger, Jude was livid. That the same people who had sat in front of him and agreed to the new strategy had then gone back to their product divisions and decided to execute their own campaigns independently was bad enough. That they had the nerve to cut their prices at the expense of the new company's well-being was beyond comprehension to him.

But what disturbed Jude most of all was the reaction of his boss, the head of marketing, and the other executives.

Nothing.

He had expected an onslaught of frustration and anger—perhaps directed at him—but experienced none of it. No phone calls, e-mails, stops by the office to ask, "what went wrong?" Nothing. *How could that be?* Jude wondered.

And that's when it dawned on him: someone up there was behind it all. The people who had come to Jude's meeting and politely nodded their heads were not to blame. They were mere minions. The real problem was at the top.

Still, Jude had to find out for himself. So he went to his boss and asked if anyone had noticed the problem, and whether they were upset. The marketing VP sighed, shook his head and explained that these kinds of redundancies and overlap were natural following a merger, and that Jude wouldn't be blamed for it.

Though he was certainly glad to be out of harm's way, relief was not Jude's dominant emotion at that moment. It was a loss of respect for management, and a nagging concern about the future of the organization.

"Maybe this is just how big companies work," he explained to an incredulous Theresa that night over dinner. "I guess I'll just keep my head down for a while, do the best I can in my piece of the world, and immerse myself even more in my extracurricular stuff," as he had come to refer to his advisory board activities.

But Jude was smart enough to realize that avoidance and denial would probably not be the best course of action for him, and that problems don't usually go away on their own. And besides, he did not have the patience to stand by and watch things unravel.

So, with the security of a nice little nest egg in hand—thanks to the rising stock price—Jude decided to go sniffing for another job.

SEEDS

Given the growing economy and his network of friends in the industry, Jude was unsurprised at how quickly he had a full slate of interviews, and at how many of them yielded offers. But what did surprise him was how much he was enjoying the job-hunting process.

Every interview gave him an opportunity to learn about another organization, another market, another set of challenges. And though he couldn't quite convince himself to join one of those companies—especially with so much Batch stock still to be vested—every time Jude turned down an offer, the seeds of a new idea started growing in his head. Realizing that he would never find the variety he wanted in a regular job, he ***began*** to wonder if he shouldn't be a consultant.

For the next couple of months Jude continued interviewing and feeding his interest in consulting. But each time he started to seriously consider it, he'd get sucked back into his day job by an urgent project, and the idea would go dormant. Jude would later refer to that nine-week period as "the longest year of my career."

And then it happened. The company's stock, defying the chaos that was driving its employees crazy, hit a level that was three times the merger price. Now Jude's nest egg began to feel like a full-grown bird; even if he didn't stay long enough for all of his options to be vested, he'd have the stock equivalent of two years' worth of salary. And so he decided the time was ripe for a change.

THE LEAP

Gingerly broaching the subject with Theresa, Jude was shocked by her reaction.

"Well, normally I would support you without reservation. You know that."

He nodded, and she continued.

"But now that I'm speaking for two of us, I'm going to have to be a little more careful."

At first it didn't occur to Jude what his wife was referring to. And then it hit him.

Theresa was pregnant.

After a half hour of quiet celebration and considerable hugging, the conversation shifted back to his career.

Theresa made the conditions of her support clear. "As long as there's a solid plan for health benefits, then I'm all for it. I know you'll do well." she assured him. "Especially if you're passionate about this."

Jude trusted his wife's instincts more than anyone's, and he could not deny his passion for what he was about to do.

So the next morning he announced to his boss that he would be leaving, and after seventy-two hours of counter-offers and hand wringing, Jude jumped.

But freedom would have its costs.

PART TWO

Roller Coaster

LOW-HANGING FRUIT

After a weeklong sabbatical during which he set up his home office and a baby's room, Jude dove into his new venture head first.

Determined to avoid the common entrepreneurial mistake of overindulging in naming his company and designing a logo (it was 1995, so a website wasn't really necessary), Jude focused his efforts instead on finding customers. Even Theresa was surprised when it took Jude just four days to fill his dance card with three paying clients, plus another pro bono.

Though he sold himself as a general consultant with expertise in marketing and operational effectiveness, it seemed clear to Jude that his ability to land clients had more to do with what he called the three Rs: his reputation, the relationships he had with executives, and the rapport he developed during sales calls.

With a slate of paying customers on board, Jude finally gave in and spent a few hours thinking about the peripheral details of the firm. Following his wife's advice, he settled on the name *Cousins Consulting*. Though not creative at first glance, it appealed to them because of its double meaning. Jude had been telling Theresa about his aspiration to have a family-like relationship with his clients. Not an immediate family member, maybe, but someone close enough be trusted. Like a cousin.

Then Theresa came up with a simple but professional logo for Jude's business cards, letterhead, and invoices. Cousins Consulting seemed official.

It wasn't the trappings of his new firm that really excited Jude, though. It was the variety of clients he would be working with.

CLIENTS

THE MADISON HOTEL

Jude's first call had been to Dante Lucca, GM of the Madison, San Francisco's oldest, largest, and most prestigious independent hotel. Jude had been a valuable and versatile member of the company's advisory board for a little over a year, and Dante was more than happy to take him on as a paid consultant.

After buying the historic but worn landmark five years earlier, Dante had overseen a massive and expensive renovation of the three-hundred-room facility, restoring it to its position as the jewel of Nob Hill. He also received some recognition within the industry for flattening the management structure of the hotel and taking a hands-on role that was rare for an owner and general manager.

For the first three years after the physical renovation and organizational restructuring, business at the Madison boomed. Recently, however, occupancy had begun to drop slightly in the face of mounting competition from upscale chain hotels. And to make matters worse, there were rumors that employees were entertaining overtures from organized labor, threatening the Madison's stature as one of the few remaining nonunion hotels in the city.

Dante hired Jude hoping he would be able to provide him with advice in the areas of market positioning and strategic clarity, and anywhere else he could add value to the hotel.

JMJ FITNESS MACHINES

Contrasting with the metropolitan world of the Madison was Jude's second client, JMJ Fitness Machines, a manufacturer of high-end consumer and institutional exercise equipment. JMJ's headquarters and manufacturing plant were located in Manteca, a small town sixty miles east of San Francisco, in the agricultural San Joaquin Valley where Jude had grown up.

The company's CEO, Brian Bailey, had been a longtime board member at Hatch, and had come to know and respect Jude during his rapid ascent there. He had even quietly tried to hire Jude at one point, though he couldn't quite convince him to move to Manteca. Still, in the course of just three or four interviews, the two developed a remarkably close relationship.

At JMJ, Brian was trying to figure out how to reduce his company's costs to compete with cheaper labor overseas, but without hurting quality or productivity. He wanted Jude to help him.

CHILDREN'S HOSPITAL

Not only did Brian hire Jude on as a consultant, he referred him to a customer and old friend. Lindsay Wagner—not to be confused with the actress who played the Bionic Woman on television—was president and CEO of the Children's Hospital of Sacramento. She had been a pediatrician for fifteen years before making the jump to administration and working her way up the corporate ladder.

Lindsay's reign as head of CHS was just four weeks old, and she wasn't initially prepared to bring on a consultant. But after a few hours with Jude, she decided he was just the kind of resource that could help her as she made the transition to her new role.

CORPUS CHRISTI CHURCH

Finally, Jude agreed to help Father Ralph Colombano, pastor at Corpus Christi Church in Walnut Creek, California. Father Ralph had married Jude and Theresa when he was a staff priest at a different parish, and had recently been assigned to run Corpus Christi.

When pressed by Theresa, Jude found it hard to decide which of his clients excited him most. The hotel would be interesting because—after years of corporate travel—he could relate to the business from a customer viewpoint. Though he had attended advisory board meetings and an occasional wedding reception there, Jude had never spent the night at the Madison and was looking forward to getting a more in-depth, behind-the-scenes look at what made the place go, or in this case, what was holding it back.

The hospital in Sacramento interested Jude for a few reasons. First, the sheer complexity of the business intrigued him. And he found the round-the-clock, mission-critical nature of the operation both fascinating and overwhelming compared to the relatively stable business of selling software. Most compelling of all, however, was the fact that Theresa was about eight months away from giving birth, and Jude was anxious to learn more about the process that she would be going through.

And of course, Jude was happy to work with Father Ralph at Corpus Christi because it would be a great opportunity to give back to the Church and to an old friend, something Jude had always wanted to do but never understood how he could contribute. On top of that, Jude had always wondered how churches operated between Monday and Saturday.

But beyond any of those clients, it was the fitness equipment company out in the valley that captured Jude's interest most of all. Not only was the business problem there a substantial one, but Jude had always been strangely fascinated by industrial manufacturing, where concepts like quality and product management seemed so much more tangible than in the world of high tech. And over the years Jude had come to admire Brian Bailey's straightforward approach to management; he was eager to see it from an inside perspective.

Exactly how Jude would ultimately add value to these clients was still somewhat unclear to him. But based on his advisory board experience and his observation of the parade of consultants hired by Hatch over the years, he was confident that he would be able to justify the cost of his services. Still, Jude wondered if he wasn't overlooking something.

CANDY

For the first three months Jude was a kid in his own little candy store. In any given week he might find himself walking the factory floor at JMJ, touring the operating room at Children's Hospital, or taking Theresa with him to do "customer research" at the Madison.

More than the novelty of these activities, Jude loved the process of observing real business problems. And trying to solve them. Whether he was talking to clients, interviewing their customers, or observing their operations, Jude was a happy man. He even admitted to enjoying their meetings. "I think I was made to be a consultant," he told his wife on more than one occasion.

As is so often the case with people who love their work, Jude succeeded wildly. In those first months alone, he found ways to make meaningful contributions to almost every one of his clients.

At the Madison, he convinced Dante to shift marketing dollars away from business travelers and focus instead on upscale leisure travelers. While large chain hotel competitors could certainly woo away executives looking for cheaper rates and more sophisticated in-room technology, Jude argued, they couldn't offer high-end visitors to San Francisco the atmosphere and uniqueness that the Madison did. Jude encouraged Dante not to compete on price but to relish his hotel's status as an upscale, even pricey, destination.

In Sacramento, Jude helped an overwhelmed Lindsay put together a simple management radar screen that she could use to monitor the success of the dozens of initiatives under way at the hospital. This allowed her to avoid spending unnecessary time on many projects that seemed urgent but weren't actually all that important. He also started doing weekly calls with her, to give her a chance to vent and talk through sensitive issues that she couldn't discuss with her staff.

Because of his fresh, naive perspective and his unabashed enthusiasm for manufacturing, Jude was able to identify a few redundant processes at JMJ that experienced plant managers had overlooked after years on the job. His willingness to ask simple—sometimes almost embarrassingly simple—questions, and his lack of condescension and pretension, earned him the trust of the factory supervisors, who were more accustomed to cocky management consultants from the high-priced Ivy League firms. As a result, they were more willing to listen to his suggestions and ideas.

As for Corpus Christi, Father Ralph had decided to wait a few months before bringing Jude in. The church was in the midst of a few personnel changes and thought it would be best to begin any new initiative after things had settled down.

All in all, Jude felt that Cousins Consulting could not have been doing any better after one quarter in business. Revenue was fairly strong. Clients seemed genuinely happy. Theresa liked her husband's more flexible schedule, especially now that she was almost halfway through her pregnancy. Jude was having the time of his life and wondering why he hadn't gone into consulting sooner.

And then life got interesting.

BREATHE

The first piece of news that Jude received was the biggest shock of all. He would never forget that moment.

He was standing next to his wife, who was lying on a table at John Muir Medical Center. As a nurse rubbed some kind of gel on Theresa's extended stomach, Jude couldn't resist analyzing the actions of the doctors and nurses around him and wondering how he might be able to help Children's Hospital become more efficient. And that's when he heard the phrase that he would never forget.

"Wow." The nurse had a tinge of shock in her voice. She was moving a wand over Theresa's midsection while looking at a monitor that neither Jude nor his wife could see.

"What's wrong?" Jude and Theresa almost shouted in unison.

The nurse frowned, focusing on the screen and slowly turned the large monitor so that the couple could see it too. Suddenly, her frown morphed delightfully into a smile. "Do you see what I see?"

Theresa and Jude studied the moving image on the green monitor, unable to understand what they were looking at. And then Theresa began to cry. "Oh my, Lord. There's two."

Now Jude looked closer and saw what his wife did. Two babies. Coming in and out of focus as they squirmed and moved. "Twins," he whispered. "Wow." He hugged his wife and wiped the tears of joy that were streaming down her face.

Jude would later describe his feelings in the moment as mostly excitement, mixed with a measure of panic. His anxiety stemmed from the realization of double-duty feedings and burpings and diaper changes. The loss of sleep that people had been predicting for him, and that he had largely waved off as hyperbole, was now starting to sound formidable.

At no time, however, did Jude even think about the financial implications of twins. Especially when everything was going so well in his new consulting practice.

INVADING THE NEST

The day of the big announcement had been a blur for Jude. Between helping Theresa deal with her own emotional roller coaster, calling family members to tell them the news, and figuring out how to transform the *baby's* room into a *babies'* room, he had no time to read the paper or watch the news. Which was why he was so surprised when he picked up the next morning's newspaper and learned about one of the largest stock market dips in five years.

The writer of the article assured investors that *"the correction was not as widespread as had once been feared."* Jude was relieved. Until he kept reading. *"The impact is being felt primarily within the high-tech community."*

Jude scanned the rest of the article and then looked at an accompanying chart on the inside page of the business section. With a chill in the pit of his stomach he read the names of the companies that had been most adversely affected. Fourth from the top was Batch. It had lost more than

30 percent of its value in one day. Jude's nest egg had shrunk considerably.

But the market has a way of rebounding after a one-day fall, and Jude was hopeful. Which was why he was so disappointed when Hatch lost another 20 percent by noon the following day.

And if that weren't bad enough, Jude found that he might have actually contributed to the exacerbation of his own financial difficulties. An article in the next day's *Wall Street Journal* profiled the companies hit hardest by the market correction. According to the story, one of the factors that pushed Batch's stock further down than most of the others in the industry was the ongoing loss of key talent just below the senior executive level, especially in engineering—and marketing.

SNOWBALL

Jude was not the kind of guy to panic about work. He had watched his father, who owned a grocery store for thirty years in Modesto, negotiate the inevitable ups and downs of being an entrepreneur. He had survived a difficult career change when he left his journalism job in Chicago to come back to California and dive into technology with no contacts or experience. And he talked Theresa into going out with him against the advice of her friends.

So Jude decided he wasn't about to let an extra baby and a financial setback get him down. But that was before he learned that Theresa would probably be having that extra baby, as well as the original one, a month ahead of schedule.

"That's pretty standard for twins," Lindsay reassured him, right before she explained that she was going to have to cut Jude's retainer in half, "at least until next year's budget gets finalized." She estimated that it would take no more than two months to wrap that up.

But then the worst news of all came.

While Jude was driving back to the Bay Area from Sacramento, Brian Bailey called. He was in a good mood.

"Jude, I just wanted to call and thank you for the work you did with the assembly team earlier this month. We're going to take what we learned there and apply it in design and procurement, and I think we'll be able to save considerable money before the end of the year. I knew you were good, but I didn't expect it to be so easy."

Jude was relieved to get some good news, until Brian continued.

"So let's wrap up your consulting gig at the end of the month. Send us any receipts that are outstanding, and we'll have you paid up on the last day."

Jude was stunned, but didn't want Brian to hear it. He responded as though he expected Brian's call all along. "No problem. I'll get everything over to you tomorrow."

Still, he wasn't about to let a client go without a fight. "I do want to ask if there is anything else you think I can do for you."

The lack of immediate response from Brian suggested that it hadn't occurred to him before, and more important for Jude, that he was considering it.

"No, I can't think of anything. Did you have something specific in mind?"

Now Jude was caught off guard, but recovered in time to come up with something. "Well, I was thinking about marketing, for one. And I'm not sure where you stand in terms of sales operations."

Brian responded immediately, and politely. "Nope. We just finished a marketing review and brought in a new guy from one of our competitors. And sales ops is already humming. I really think we're doing fine in those areas."

The last thing Jude wanted to convey was desperation, so with an air of confidence bordering on indifference, he closed the conversation. "Great. Let me know if there is anything else I can do for you."

"I'll certainly do that. You did a great job for us. And keep in touch."

Jude assured him that he would, hung up the phone, and decided that maybe this consulting thing wasn't such a good idea after all.

ANALYSIS

The way Jude saw it, he had two problems. First, he needed more clients. That was a no-brainer. Though he had enough money to pay the bills for six months, beyond that he had been counting on the Batch stock to rebound, a hope that was fading a little more every day.

Second, he needed something to sell to those clients. As obvious as that seemed, up until now Jude hadn't felt the need to be so specific. As an advisory board member, he didn't have to focus his advice in one particular area. And he certainly had no trouble landing his clients—not to mention adding value to them—without a clear service offering, other than a general aptitude in marketing and operations. But he never suspected that *keeping* those clients would require an explicitly defined program.

Even as a marketing executive, Jude had prided himself on being something of a generalist. He thought that his well-roundedness would serve him well as a consultant, allowing him to avoid being pigeonholed. Suddenly he was desperate for a pigeonhole, but he couldn't seem to find one.

After a week of painfully unproductive brain-racking, Jude was beginning to feel that he had made a mistake. *I'm going to be providing for a four-person family soon. Am I crazy?* Deciding to give up, he broke the news to his wife over dinner.

SECOND WIND

Theresa would hear none of it. "Come on. Tell me that you haven't enjoyed working more during the past few months than in the last five years combined," she told her husband.

Jude admitted it was true, but countered, "Yeah, I'd probably like being a cowboy too, but that doesn't mean it's what I should do."

"That's not true."

Jude was confused. "So you think I should be a—"

"You'd be a miserable cowboy." She smiled, forcing a laugh from her husband.

"But you're a great consultant. You said it yourself, you were made to be one. Just because you've had an early setback doesn't mean you should go back to Hatch or Batch or whatever it's called now with your tail between your legs."

He gladly agreed with his wife and decided to rededicate himself to making his consulting practice work. Little did he know that he would be back at Batch sooner than he expected.

EXPLORATION

Determined to power through the problem, Jude did what he would advise any other businessperson to do. He asked his customers what they wanted.

What really kept them up at night? What made them mad? What made them want to quit sometimes? What they would give their left leg to change?

He talked to Lindsay, Brian, Dante, even Father Ralph, as well as a handful of other executives he knew. He recorded the conversations and took as many notes as he could. He listened to the tapes and pored through his notebooks, looking for something that would qualify as a compelling, universal need.

A few of the executives mentioned quality. Most didn't.

Two of them talked about labor problems. But that was largely a union issue for the hospital, and a concern for Dante if things didn't go well at the hotel.

And all of them referred to technology challenges, but they already had plenty of consultants focused on that, and Jude was neither skilled at nor interested in doing technical work.

It was only when Jude was going through his notes for the third time that he spotted it.

"Of course," he murmured to himself. "There it is."

DISCOVERY

Dante had mentioned it twice. Lindsay referred to it using a variety of terms on three different occasions. Father Ralph almost used a curse word when he mentioned it. A number of the others had called it by name. Everyone but Brian had complained about it at one time or another.

Silos.

Some called it *departmental politics,* or *infighting,* or *lack of divisional cooperation.* But as he thought back on those interviews, almost every one of them used the *silo* word at some point during the conversation.

Lindsay described the problem at Children's Hospital where doctors and staff members seemed to be almost at war at times. At his hotel, Dante couldn't get the front office staff to cooperate with housekeeping and maintenance. Father Ralph surprised him most of all when he explained that the Parish Council and the Parent-Teacher Committee were at odds over how to use the school facilities during weekends.

And then Jude thought about Batch. Headquarters versus the field. Sales versus engineering. Hatch versus Bell. Silos.

It had been right in front of him all along, and yet he hadn't realized just how universal the problem was, and how much pain it caused CEOs and their companies. Slowly, Jude was convincing himself that this silo thing was exactly the issue around which he needed to build his practice.

Now all he had to do was find a solution to the silo problem—something he felt confident he could do given his experience at Batch—and convince his clients to give him a chance to help them implement it. The second part of the challenge seemed like it would be more difficult, so Jude decided to start there.

SALES

Jude's first call was to Dante Lucca. He was still a paying client, and so Jude felt like he could more confidently sell him on the idea to see how he would react.

"Are you kidding?" the hotelier responded. "If you can help me get these people to work together, I'll double your retainer."

Jude hoped Dante was serious about that statement.

Lindsay at Children's Hospital was no less enthusiastic than Dante, but was still hampered by her financial planning process. "I would love nothing more than to have you help us deal with the rift between doctors and nurses and admittance. But first I have to get my budget finalized and approved." Then she paused, reconsidering. "You know, I'm the CEO of this darn hospital. Let me see if I can shift around some discretionary funds so you can start sooner. Give me three weeks to figure it out."

Notwithstanding the delay at the hospital, Jude felt like he had hit the jackpot with the silo issue. But he needed at least one more client. He considered calling Brian at JMJ Fitness, and then decided against it. *He didn't mention anything about silos,* he reasoned.

Then something occurred to Jude that was either complete genius or stupidity. *What about Batch?*

On one hand, there was no doubt that the company had problems with departmental infighting. And Jude knew the organization inside and out.

On the other hand, the executives were probably not too happy with Jude, especially after the infamous newspaper story about the brain drain at the company. And even if they could see beyond that, would they view Jude as being credible? Or would he be an insider, a prophet in his own back yard?

Torn, Jude turned to Theresa.

"You should definitely talk to them. What's the worst that can happen?"

Jude winced. "They can strip me of any semblance of self-esteem that I have left, that's what can happen!"

Theresa smiled, knowing her husband's sometimes morose sense of humor. "Okay, but other than that?"

Now Jude laughed. "I know. I know. All they can say is no. They probably won't even laugh in front of me. They'll wait until I leave."

"I don't think they'll laugh at you. In fact, I think there is a better than 75 percent chance they'll hire you."

"How can you say that? Did you forget that I quit? And

now they're in the toilet financially. Don't you think they're going to be just a little pissed at me?"

Theresa shook her head emphatically. "No. I think they're going to see you in a different light now. You're an outsider. And remember, you broke up with *them*. Having you back, even as a consultant, would probably be somewhat redemptive. And misery loves company."

Jude thought about it for a moment. "I don't know."

"Come on. I'll bet you fifty bucks they say yes."

Slowly, Jude seemed to be warming up to the idea. "You know, I'm sure Brian Bailey would be willing to tell them how I helped him at JMJ."

Sensing an opening, Theresa pushed a little further. "And you've got nothing to lose."

"Other than my self-esteem." Jude countered.

"And fifty dollars."

PUSHING FORWARD

Jude was surprised that he had little trouble scheduling a meeting with Carter Bell.

Because he hadn't really forged a personal relationship with the new CEO before leaving the company, Jude was taken aback by Carter's warm response and apparent enthusiasm during their brief telephone call. This certainly wasn't the brash caricature of a man that he had expected. Jude wondered if the company's recent slide had humbled him a little.

And though he couldn't decide whether it was Brian's recommendation that opened the door for him, or if Theresa's theory about misery loving company was correct, Jude was already starting to feel like there was a chance he might lose his $50 bet.

Unfortunately, as quickly as Jude was able to arrange the meeting, it wouldn't take place for ten days because Carter was leaving for an analyst road show to convince industry experts and investors that the company was headed in the right direction.

Undeterred, Jude decided that the time lag would give him a chance to develop and test a solution to the silo problem. He would start at the Madison.

After giving the situation a good deal of thought, Jude decided to propose to Dante a two-pronged approach to breaking down the barriers between the facilities department, which included housekeeping and maintenance, and the guest services group, comprising everyone from the valets, bell staff, and concierge team to the clerks checking people in and out of the hotel at the front desk.

Part one of the proposal would be a partial redesign of the compensation plans for the departments, placing greater emphasis on hotel-wide goals like customer satisfaction, and on overall company performance, revenue, and profitability. Jude had little trouble convincing Dante and his human resources director to do this. In fact, they thought it was a great idea. Though he didn't say so, Jude couldn't believe they hadn't considered it before.

The second part of the proposal would involve a session with as many of the employees from the two departments as possible. This was also an easy sell. But implementation would be a different story entirely.

TRIAL RUN

Sixty-five employees representing the two divisions streamed into one of the medium-sized banquet rooms on the first floor of the Madison. (A handful couldn't attend because they had to keep the place running.) As they settled in, Jude was surprised at how congenial the mood in the room was. People were laughing and interacting with one another as though they were about to see a movie. It wouldn't last.

Flanked by his director of facilities, who oversaw housekeeping and maintenance services, and his front office VP, who managed everything from the front desk staff and reservations agents to the concierges and bell staff, Dante kicked off the session. "The reason we're here today is to improve the working relationship between our departments. We're not here to point fingers or rehash the past, but rather to create a better experience for our guests, and for ourselves, by breaking down any barriers that might be holding us back."

Though everyone was certainly paying attention to their owner and GM, no one reacted in the slightest. Dante then introduced his consultant.

"Jude Cousins has been a member of our advisory board for a few years, and he's going to be leading today's session. I'm sure that this is going to be a productive and fun exercise." Dante's tone of voice didn't really indicate that he was *sure* of that, but rather that he merely hoped it would be true.

With that, Dante and his executives left the room, turning control over to Jude.

As soon as they were gone, Jude noticed a subtle but undeniable change in the body language and facial expressions of the employees seated in front of him. Beyond the handful of people he caught rolling their eyes in mild disgust after their leaders left, he was most surprised by the sudden lack of attention and respect that they seemed to be giving him.

Feeling like a sheep thrown to wolves—or a substitute teacher left alone with a roomful of angry fifth graders—Jude knew that if he didn't get things started quickly and compellingly, he might be eaten alive.

EXERCISE

Jude kicked things off by doing something that he hated to do, but that he thought was critical for what he was trying to accomplish. "Okay, I'd like half of the people in the room to switch tables with someone from another department. I don't want you all sitting with people you work with. That means half of the room should be getting up and moving to another table."

At first no one moved.

"Come on, I'm serious. Choose two or three people at your table to move, and have them take their stuff with them."

Slowly, people started to stand and gather their things. After almost five minutes of minor chaos, the room had been rearranged and Jude was ready to go, albeit with a little less credibility after pushing them outside their comfort zones so quickly.

"Okay, I realize that many of you already know each other, but I'd like to take the next 15 minutes to have you introduce yourselves. But rather than just saying your name and job title, I want you to answer one more question: What's the worst job you've ever had?"

He paused to let it sink in. "But it can't be the one you have now."

Everyone laughed.

"Okay, go ahead and get started."

Again, it took some time for people to warm up, but within minutes the room was buzzing with discussion and more than occasional laughter. Jude was feeling pretty good about the situation, but he knew he was barely out of the starting gate.

When everyone finished their discussions, Jude gave them their next instructions.

"Now, I'd like each table to take a half hour to come up with a list of all the things that prevent you from doing your jobs the best way that you know how. It could be anything and everything. And don't worry about editing or categorizing your answers. I don't care if it's apples, oranges, pears, or monkeys. Just get it all on the flip charts."

He motioned to the easels spread around the room. "Appoint someone on your team to do the writing, and someone else to be your spokesperson when you're done."

More interaction and laughter ensued, and Jude would have bet all the money in his wallet that the silo problem at the Madison had been overblown. He would have lost that bet.

When the flip-charting had ceased, Jude went to each of the tables and asked the spokesperson to report their findings, and ten minutes later he had a list of two dozen issues taped to the walls. It had been less than an hour since the session began, and the group had already identified their problems.

Jude then called for a break and spent the next few minutes grouping the various issues into five natural categories.

1. Excessive delays in getting rooms clean for arriving guests
2. Bad information from the front desk about priorities for guest rooms
3. Last-minute surprises about large groups checking into the hotel at the same time
4. Unwillingness of front desk and concierge employees to pitch in outside their specific job responsibilities during busy times
5. Poor treatment of housekeeping staff by front desk crew

As Jude looked at the list he'd created, it became clear that the battle lines for the next part of the session had been drawn.

DIVISION

When the room filled up again following the break, Jude noticed something that he hadn't expected: everyone was back in their original seats.

The housekeepers were sitting together, as were the bell staff and the front desk clerks and the concierges. As much as he didn't want to, Jude made them return to the tables where they were sitting before the break, something that they found even less appealing this time.

By the time they were reseated, he noticed that almost everyone in the room was already reading his five-point summary. Thankfully, many of them were nodding as if to say *that's right. Those are the issues.*

And so he began. "Are there any questions about this before we start the next part of today's session? Because what we're going to do now is focus on finding solutions to these problems." Just as he was about to move on, a lone hand in the back of the room went up.

It was a front desk supervisor, a tall woman with her blonde hair tied up in a tight bun. "Are you going to let us pick which of these issues we work on?" She didn't wait for an answer. "Because I'd like to do the first one," she said, referring to the slow turnaround of clean rooms.

Jude noticed more than a few of the housekeepers rolling their eyes.

"No. I'm going to assign the issues randomly to your tables, so that we give every issue attention." He then made the assignments.

For the next half hour, employees brainstormed solutions to the various problems. Jude encouraged everyone to weigh in, even if their jobs were not directly related to the issues being discussed.

When it came time to report back, the results were not pretty.

Regardless of where they were seated, it seemed as though housekeepers only saw the world from a housekeeping perspective, front desk clerks from a front desk perspective, and so on. And no one was terribly diplomatic.

At one point, a front desk supervisor actually suggested that the hotel replace many of the housekeeping staff and hire "hungrier" people for the job. A concierge recommended that the housekeeping and maintenance staffs be reorganized and report directly to the head of the front desk. This was met by a smattering of boos from some of the housekeepers in the room, and prompted a maintenance worker to complain that the bell staff called the housekeepers maids, or worse yet, *toilet scrubbers*.

Everyone pointed a finger at one of the other departments, convinced that they were the cause of the hotel's problems, and that they only cared about their own part of the hotel and nothing beyond.

At this point, Jude certainly had a vivid picture of the silo problem. Unfortunately, the session so far had only served to reinforce the barriers between the departments, and Jude needed to salvage the day. So he took a risk.

ROLE PLAY

"I want everyone to go back to your original tables and sit with the people you work with," he said. This time he didn't have to urge them to move. When they were settled, he explained the next exercise.

"I want you," he pointed at a table full of bell staff, "to pretend that you're housekeepers." One of the older ladies in the back of the room yelled, "You mean maids!" The room burst out into laughter.

Then he pointed to another table, this one filled with housekeepers. "And I want you to pretend that you work at the front desk."

One by one he went to each table assigning them a role that would be particularly different for them than their regular jobs. Then he explained. "When I call on you, I want each table to be as stereotypical as possible about describing the problems from your perspective. But play it straight. I want you to really assume the roles I've given you."

Nervous laughter filled the room.

Jude pointed to the housekeepers who had been assigned front desk roles. "What is the problem around here?"

After a brief pause, one of them spoke up. "Those housekeepers are just too slow and lazy. They don't care about guests. All they want to do is get through the day and get home. They don't understand the pressure we're under down here."

A number of people laughed, and a few even applauded, at the accurate depiction of what a front desk clerk would probably say.

Jude couldn't turn back now. "What about you housekeepers?" He pointed to the table full of bell staff.

A tall young man with a goatee spoke with an affected feminine voice, playfully mimicking a housekeeper. "Yeah, but why should we work hard, anyway. We don't get many tips. And even if we bust our butts and turn our rooms around quickly, no one really appreciates us. It's no wonder two of our best housekeepers left last month. And no one ever helps us. You'd think one of the guys in the monkey suits standing downstairs might come upstairs every once in a while and vacuum or something."

The room howled with laughter, and the housekeepers burst into spontaneous applause.

Jude pushed on, looking at a table full of maintenance workers pretending to be concierges. "What do you think is the real problem?"

After a considerable delay, one of the older guys spoke up, nervously. "Well, we sit down here in the lobby and watch the whole operation, and we think the problem is all about communication."

"What do you mean?" Jude asked.

"Well, those front desk clerks," he pointed to the table full of housekeepers, "they don't talk to the people upstairs, the housekeepers, until there's an emergency. And by then, it's too late. And when the emergency's over, they don't even think to go upstairs and say thank you. It's like they're too good or something."

The maintenance man paused, and then continued with more passion.

"And when they call the maintenance guys to fix a toilet or something, they act like they're second-class citizens. I mean, it's bad enough that we, I mean they, have to fix toilets. It only makes it worse when they look down at them. Heck, we're the ones who have to keep this beautiful hotel in good shape."

No one laughed this time. The maintenance man blushed.

Jude thanked him, and continued going around the room until every table had a few opportunities to speak. When he finished, he asked a question he hoped someone would answer.

"So, what do you guys think about all this?"

Silence.

Until one of the housekeepers, a Hispanic woman named Estela, raised her hand and waited to be called on.

When Jude nodded to her, she explained. "Actually I think we're all trying pretty hard."

That was it. And it was enough.

Jude looked at his watch and realized that he was ten minutes over his allotted time. He thanked everyone for their patience and participation, and assured them he would be sharing his observations with the executive team the following day.

As the room emptied, Jude couldn't deny that there was a sense of goodwill in the air that he attributed to more than just relief that the session had ended. Still, he didn't have as much information as he wanted, so he asked the managers of the various subdepartments to stay behind for a few minutes.

The four supervisors overseeing housekeeping, maintenance, the front desk clerks, and the concierges and bell staff moved to the table at the front of the room. When everyone else had gone and the doors were closed, Jude began.

"So what exactly is going on around here?"

HIGHER-UPS

After a pause, the front desk supervisor spoke. "Basically, a lot of these people just don't like each other. I mean, the facilities people upstairs come from very different backgrounds than the guest services people down here, and they have different interests. It's the same in every hotel I've worked at."

The housekeeping supervisor nodded her head in agreement, although Jude wasn't sure she really believed it.

The head concierge was shaking his head. "Wait a minute. I've worked at hotels where there wasn't so much tension between the departments. And I don't think this is about people not getting along or being different. Hell, half of my bellmen play soccer with the maintenance guys on the weekends."

"So what's the problem, then?" Jude wanted to know.

The concierge shrugged. "I honestly don't know."

Jude looked up at the list of topics written on the flipchart. "Okay, let's take one of these issues. How about last-minute surprises around large groups coming into the hotel. What's causing that?"

The front desk supervisor didn't hesitate. "Well, we used to have all-staff meetings prior the arrival of a big group, and that gave everyone a chance to ask questions and hear from Dante and the other executives. But about six months ago we stopped doing that."

Jude was curious. "Why?"

The front desk supervisor shook her head. "I'm not sure."

"I am." It was the concierge supervisor again. "People complained about them, and so Dante decided to let each department do their own updates."

"Who complained?" Jude wanted to know.

The concierge hesitated before answering. "Well, I should probably take the Fifth on that one." He looked at his peers as if he wanted their approval. "Let's just say that it wasn't us, and leave it at that."

As much as Jude wanted to say, "Who, then?" he backed off, guessing that it was someone on Dante's staff.

Looking at the list again, he asked, "Where does the lack of respect issue come from? And how big of a problem is it?"

The maintenance supervisor responded first this time. "I think it's fairly typical for the guest services people downstairs to see us," he motioned to himself and the head of housekeeping, "as being less important than they are. It's not good, but it's not completely unique to the Madison."

"And what about the less-than-flattering terms people use to describe one another."

The maintenance head laughed. "I think that's pretty standard too."

The front desk supervisor nodded in agreement. "But there is one difference here."

"What's that?" Jude wanted to know.

"Now *I'm* going to take the Fifth." Everyone laughed.

"Come on. Give me something," Jude urged them.

The head of housekeeping said cautiously, "Let's just say that those terms aren't only used by employees." Again Jude decided not to push further.

Changing the subject, he asked the big question: "Why is customer satisfaction falling?"

"Isn't it obvious?" the concierge countered. "If the bell staff and the front desk people and the housekeepers and the maintenance guys aren't communicating with each other, don't you think that the guests are going to notice? Rooms aren't ready on time because no one downstairs tells anyone upstairs which rooms they need first. Someone's TV isn't working and they call the front desk to complain. And when the maintenance guy can't get there in less than three minutes, the guest calls back to the front desk and the clerk down there blames the maintenance guy, which makes all of us look terrible. You can't hide this stuff from guests. They're going to notice."

No one argued with the monologue.

The maintenance supervisor jumped in. "And then the CFO tells us to cut the number of maintenance guys we have, to reduce costs, and the assistant general manager wants us to reduce the amount of time it takes to respond to a guest issue. And of course, Dante tells us to take as much time with the guest as possible to ensure that the problem is addressed and that they're happy. And at the end of the day all we get is grief from the front desk about why we aren't doing enough. I'm about to lose my third employee this year because of this."

"Who's leaving?" the front desk manager wanted to know.

"Raymond."

"Not Raymond. He's your best guy up there."

"The best ones always leave first," the concierge replied, resignedly.

Jude felt he finally had enough information. So he thanked everyone for staying behind to help him, and left for home.

That night he went through his notes and put together a summary of his observations and a handful of specific recommendations for addressing the issues that separated the departments and kept them from working together. As good as Jude felt about the recommendations he would make to Dante and his team the next day, he was anxious about how to present it to them, and how it would be received.

BLOW UP

When he arrived for the meeting, the hotel's executive team greeted Jude warmly.

Dante was smiling. "I heard things went well yesterday."

His assistant general manager chimed in. "Everyone I talked to really enjoyed the session. Even the cynical bellmen said it wasn't bad. And coming from them, that's a huge compliment."

Jude was now feeling a little more confident in what he was about to do. After a few minutes of polite banter, he went to the flip chart at the front of the room and began his presentation.

"I don't want to take up too much of your time today. I'll just quickly summarize what I saw yesterday and what I think can be done to improve the cooperation between facilities and the guest services group."

The executives seemed ready and eager to listen, so he dove right in. "The first thing I'd like to say is that there is definitely a problem between the departments, and it's hurting the hotel and will continue to do so if you don't do something about it."

In a subtle but undeniable way, the mood in the room shifted. Curiosity and openness on the faces of most of the executives seemed to transform into mild defensiveness.

Only Dante seemed to be excited by Jude's declaration. "Tell us what you think is causing this."

Clearing his throat, Jude explained. "Well, for one, it seems like they're receiving different messages from you about what's important." He hoped that would be enough. It wasn't.

"What kind of messages?" the front office VP asked in a way that indicated she wasn't going to be open to whatever the answer was.

Jude decided to start with the least inflammatory examples. "Like the issue of late checkouts versus getting people in their rooms when they arrive. Front desk people don't seem to know where to draw the line around that issue, and the housekeeping folks are put into a lose-lose situation."

"I don't think that's necessarily fair." She responded as soon as Jude had finished. "My people know what their priorities are. That sounds like an excuse from the housekeepers more than anything." She seemed to suddenly realize how defensive she sounded. "But I suppose it wouldn't hurt to clarify things a little." She didn't sound like she meant it.

The head of facilities winced a little at her remarks. "I don't know. I think that there's more confusion than you might be aware of. We'd certainly like your front desk people to stop telling everyone they can stay as long as they like. I mean, we have to decide who we're more willing to piss off. A guest arriving or one leaving. We can't perform miracles up there."

The front desk VP seemed ready to launch into an argument with her colleague, then turned to Jude. "Anything else?"

Jude looked at his notes. "Well, there are a few dozen issues actually. Where do you want me to start?"

Dante jumped in. "I'd like to hear more specifically about how you see all of this hurting the hotel."

Jude took a breath. "Well, for one, you've lost some key employees, which is stretching people too far and sending a bad message to everyone left behind."

No one commented, so he continued.

"It's also creating a great opportunity for the unions to move in. I mean, if your employees don't feel any sense of unity or commitment to each other, they're going to be more likely to look for it somewhere else."

Jude still couldn't tell exactly what the executives were thinking. He decided they were either in disagreement with what he was saying, or disappointed at the environment they had allowed to take root.

He pressed on. "And of course, there's the guests. As the managers told me yesterday, it's impossible for all of this not to affect them. I don't think you're going to fix your satisfaction problem until you get your people working together."

In a slightly challenging tone, the CFO asked Jude, "So what do you recommend?"

Jude hesitated, looking down at his notes. "Well, the first thing you might want to consider is try a job rotation program."

A few of the executives were frowning now, which Jude mistakenly interpreted as a sign that they didn't understand what he meant. "If you give people a chance to spend time doing one another's jobs, then they'll—"

Dante interrupted. "Yeah, we understand the idea. We tried it last year."

Jude was surprised. "How did it work?"

The front desk VP answered somewhat sarcastically. "Well, based on what you learned yesterday, how do you think it worked?"

Dante broke in to clarify the issue. "Actually, I think it was pretty well received," he said. "But obviously it didn't change behaviors. What else do you think we need to do?"

"I think you should rethink your orientation program for new employees. Provide a better understanding of how the hotel works from a bigger-picture perspective. Give everyone a sense of how they contribute to the whole operation."

No one seemed particularly impressed by the idea, though the head of HR wrote it down.

Jude continued. "And I'd recommend going back to having all-hands meetings, especially around big groups. I'm kind of surprised that you stopped doing that."

The room groaned.

The head of facilities explained. "We just didn't think it was helpful anymore."

"Why not?"

"I think we just felt like we could do it within our own departments, and that we didn't need to waste everyone's time pulling together a large meeting." He seemed less than convinced about his rationale.

"You have anything else for us?" This time it wasn't Dante, but his CFO, who was asking. His tone seemed to suggest that nothing mentioned so far had been particularly insightful.

"Have you ever considered pooling tips and sharing them with people in supporting roles?"

The reaction from the executives—a mixture of laughter and rolling eyes—made Jude feel like he had just asked a group of college deans to consider revoking tenure among their professors.

Slightly wounded and embarrassed, Jude decided to try to convince them anyway. "It just seems to me that there are plenty of people in the hotel who make a big difference to customer satisfaction and don't get much of a bonus for day-to-day heroics. When they see others doing the same amount of work, or less, and getting rewarded for it, I can see how they'd get discouraged a little."

Dante shook his head. "Sorry, my friend. That's been a problem in this industry since money was invented, and it's not something we're prepared to take on right now."

The CFO looked to Dante and jokingly asked, "How much are we paying this guy, anyway?"

The head of facilities piled on. "Are we actually paying him? I thought this was free." Everyone laughed.

Though he knew they were just teasing him, Jude felt stung enough by their remarks that he needed to respond. Letting his pride get the best of him, he made a decision that he would regret.

"There is actually another issue that we haven't talked about yet, but that I think may lie at the heart of your silo problem." He paused. "And it has to do with you."

That got everyone's attention. Any lingering smiles from those who had been teasing Jude began to fade.

"I think you could set a better example for everyone in terms of how the departments interact."

That was just too theoretical for Dante. "Set an example? How so?"

"Well, for one, it would probably be a pretty good idea if no one in this room was ever heard to call the facilities crew 'the toilet scrubbers.'"

Two of the executives tried to avoid laughing, while the others seemed embarrassed.

The front office vice president was bordering on incredulous. "Don't take this wrong, but you used more than a hundred man-hours of our employees' time yesterday, and your recommendation is that we stop calling each other names? I certainly hope we're not paying you too much." She smiled as though she were suddenly trying to twist her insult into a joke, but no one bought it. And they certainly weren't laughing.

Jude was about to respond by pointing out that it was only one of four recommendations he had made and that he had seven more pages of notes outlining the problems at the hotel and that if the executive team didn't want to hear anything that they might be doing wrong then maybe they shouldn't have asked him to. . . .

But before he could say a word, Dante jumped in.

"Listen, I think Jude makes a good point here. It would be a good idea if all of us were more careful about the things we said in front of our employees. Even though we all get along fine and know that we're just joking with one another, it can send a bad message."

No one responded.

Dante decided to bring the entire session to an early close. "I want to thank Jude for his time and effort yesterday, and recommend that we take a good look at his suggestions. Getting an outside perspective on our problems, even if it merely confirms what we already know, is helpful."

Ouch. Jude would have preferred that Dante had just said, "Okay, this wasn't very insightful or useful, and frankly, we're not going to be implementing any of it. But thanks anyway." And while he understood that Dante wanted to rescue his consultant from a school of sharks smelling blood in the water, he would have liked him to show a little more support for him while the front office VP was taking potshots.

As the executives filed past him and out the door, Jude felt a bizarre sense of failure, one that he had never experienced as a professional.

FALL OUT

When everyone else had left, Dante shut the door and turned toward Jude, smiling in a forced kind of way. "Well, that was certainly interesting."

They laughed a little painfully.

Jude felt a mix of emotions. First, he was frustrated by the team's immaturity. He also felt a little betrayed by Dante for not allowing him to address the defensive barrage he had just received, though he certainly understood his motivation for ending the discussion. But more than anything else, he was embarrassed.

"Listen, Dante, I'm sorry that I—"

Dante held up his hand. "Don't apologize. It's fine." He took a breath as he considered the situation. "I mean, I wish you would have brought up the executive name calling stuff earlier, because it sounded like you were sandbagging us a little. But we needed to hear those things, and some of my staff members were way out of line. I'll talk to them about it."

Though he felt better, Jude couldn't help but consider the implications. "I can't possibly have credibility with your team now, can I? I'd understand if you ended our agreement."

Dante shook his head. "Listen, I don't want to overdramatize what just happened. But I'm also not going to lie to you. This is the team that I have to work with every day, and you're just a consultant. So if push comes to shove. . . . " He didn't finish. "But you've still got a few weeks left on your retainer, right?"

Jude nodded.

"Let's take a look at the situation then, when things calm down." Dante patted Jude on the back and walked him to the front door of the hotel. "You gave me some things to think about today."

Jude thanked his client and went home, more than a little concerned about the future of his business—and his family's financial situation. He couldn't deny that he was desperate. But desperation is sometimes a great motivator.

PART THREE

Rally

THE DRAWING BOARD

One week. That's all the time Jude had to make a breakthrough because that's when his next workshop was scheduled to take place at Children's Hospital. He immediately became almost obsessed with figuring out the "silo thing," as he and Theresa came to refer to it, reading everything he could get his hands on having anything to do with organizational politics.

But Jude would not find his answer in any book. It would find him, in a more frightening way that he could ever have imagined.

ALARM

Jude did not sleep much after the debacle at the Madison. In fact, he had not been sleeping well ever since Brian called to announce an end to his consulting assignment at JMJ. Now, in addition to his financial worries, Jude couldn't stop thinking about the silo problem. Add to that his wife's growing discomfort at night, and it wasn't much of a surprise that Jude was awake when it all started happening.

It was 4:32 A.M. Jude would not forget that. Theresa had been shifting and groaning off and on throughout the night, which wasn't completely new given the size of the babies inside her and their increasing penchant for kicking. But something was different on this night, and more than an hour before Jude's alarm usually rang, Theresa sat up in bed, wincing in pain.

"Are you okay?" Jude asked.

Theresa nodded. "Yeah, I think so." She wasn't convincing.

And then they saw blood on the sheets.

Realizing that she was in no position to walk, Jude called 911—and said a prayer while they waited.

Seven minutes later the ambulance was out front, and twelve minutes later they were well on their way to John Muir Medical Center, which was just eight miles from the Cousins' new home.

For a moment Jude wondered how he and Theresa would get home from the hospital, given that they were arriving in an ambulance. But his logistical concern disappeared when Theresa's pain increased. As the EMT ministered to Theresa, Jude held her hand and smiled, trying to reassure her.

In minutes, they arrived at the emergency room, and the EMTs rolled Theresa through the wide doors, where they were greeted by two nurses and an administrative attendant of some kind.

Jude described to them what had been happening, and the administrative person asked him questions about Theresa's condition and personal information. Name, address, insurance, and related issues.

Theresa was now in the ER, where doctors and nurses were calmly but intensely sprinting around, taking her temperature and pulse and a dozen other diagnostics related to her and the babies. All the while, a nurse was explaining to Jude what was happening, though he wasn't digesting much of it, lost instead in watching his wife's face and praying harder than he had ever prayed in his life. And then the doctor turned away from Theresa to speak to her husband.

"She's fine for now, and the babies are too. But I'm calling in Dr. Andrew Luke from the birthing center to take over. He's on site and will have a better idea of what to do."

Without having to be told, one of the nurses was on the phone and Jude could hear her. "Hi, this is Jean down in ER. We need Luke right away. We've got a woman a little over seven months pregnant with mild bleeding. Thanks."

Five minutes later Dr. Luke arrived. He spoke to the ER doctor for a minute, and then went right over to his new patient.

"Hi, Theresa." Smiling at her and taking her hand, he looked over at the babies' heart monitors and the ultrasound computer screen that had just been set up. After no more than fifteen seconds, he nodded his head at Theresa and looked around the room, settling on Jude.

"Are you her husband?"

Jude nodded but couldn't seem to say anything.

In a quick but reassuring way, he explained, "I'm Dr. Luke. Everything looks fine right now. But we're going to take your wife to surgery just in case."

"In case what?" Jude asked, a little more abruptly than he had intended.

"In case we can't keep the babies from coming."

Jude froze. "You mean from being born?"

Dr. Luke smiled, and then turned toward one of the nurses. "Let's get into the O.R. right away." One of them went to make a phone call, while another logged on to a computer. "And call Dr. Schmitz and ask him to meet me there in ten minutes."

As people scattered, one of the nurses yelled across the room with an edge to her voice, "Janet, get back over here! We need to order a magnesium drip and start a new IV!" Jude looked over to where the nurse had yelled, and saw another nurse, who most certainly was Janet. Without the slightest reaction to the abrupt order, she quickly and unceremoniously made a telephone call, apparently to the O.R., while simultaneously preparing some sort of document.

"What's a magnesium drip?" He asked the question to no one in particular.

As Janet hung up the phone, she calmly explained that it was something that could help a woman hold off giving birth.

Within minutes two nurses or orderlies—Jude didn't know what the terms really meant—came into the room, moved Theresa onto a gurney, and began to roll her toward an exit in the emergency room. At the door, a man dressed like a security guard took over for one of the nurses, who disappeared after brushing Theresa's hair from her eyes and saying, "You're going to be fine."

Before Jude knew what was happening, two more nurses appeared, one of whom was monitoring a machine that they rolled beside Theresa, while the other was filling out forms and directing what little traffic was in the hallways at 5:15 A.M.

Jude quickly moved alongside his wife's entourage to be with her as they proceeded down the hallway. He held her hand as they gracefully and speedily moved her to the elevators, then up to the fourth floor and over to the birthing center.

As they emerged through the doors, a nurse dressed in a flowery pink blouse greeted them, smiling. "Hello there, Theresa. You doing okay?"

Jude watched as his wife, in pain, smiled and nodded her head at the matronly yet angelic nurse. *Who is this wonderful woman?* Jude remembered wondering for a split second before being led to the doorway just outside the operating room, where he was stunned by the bright lights and relative starkness of the facility there. After changing into his surgical scrubs, he was inside the operating room and with Theresa again.

A long minute later Dr. Luke entered, now dressed for surgery. Ignoring Jude for the most part, he went straight to Theresa, smiled at her in a way that said "I'm excited to be here with you," and turned to one of his nurses and asked, "Has Dr. Schmitz arrived yet?"

At that very moment another man entered. His hair was disheveled, and he was wearing a different color outfit from the others. They smiled at one another before Dr. Luke replied, "Well, here he is now."

"Hey there, Andy," Dr. Luke greeted his colleague before turning to Theresa. "And how are you doing?"

Looking no more disheveled than Dr. Schmitz, Theresa smiled back at him. “I'm okay.”

“Well, you're about to have two little girls.”

“But I'm only seven and a half months—”

He interrupted her, smiling. “We do this all the time.” He patted her hand, asked the nurse to call the anesthesiologist, and the process began.

REGROUP

At 5:45 A.M., Dr. Luke and Dr. Schmitz delivered the tiny Cousins twins, doing a Cesarean section. Nurses quickly cleaned up the three-pound babies and took them immediately to the Neonatal Intensive Care Unit next door.

Dr. Luke and Dr. Schmitz assured the parents that all had gone well, and that they'd be able to see the babies shortly. Theresa was wheeled off to the recovery room, and as soon as she was gone, Jude fell into a chair outside the NICU. He looked at his watch, which read 5:57 A.M.

He was amazed. Everything, from the moment they woke up in bed until now, had happened in less than ninety minutes. Life would never be the same.

HURRY UP AND WAIT

For the next three days, Theresa remained hospitalized just fifty feet from where her babies, Hailey and Emily, were being watched around the clock.

Her pediatrician and the head of the NICU explained that the babies would have to stay for at least three weeks. During that time, parents were encouraged to come in and touch them for a few hours a day, but given the girls' early arrival, they wouldn't be ready to be held or fed like later-term babies for a week or so. Even then, there was only so much Theresa and Jude would be able to do. The thought of being at home without the girls was an unpleasant one for the new parents.

When it came time for Theresa to be discharged from the hospital, there was confusion as to which department was responsible for releasing her, and who would be billing the insurance company for what. Given Theresa's emotional and physical exhaustion, this was particularly trying for her, and she was cranky about the chaos. After more than an hour of delays and phone calls, she was finally cleared to leave.

When he and Theresa arrived home and caught their breath, Jude quickly came to the conclusion that he should work as much as he could while the girls were in the hospital, both to take his mind off his worries about them and to get his business on track so that he could spare a little more time when they finally did come home. And besides, Theresa's mother would be staying with them for the next month, so there really wasn't much to do around the house until the babies arrived.

Jude had originally postponed his session at Children's Hospital when the girls were born. Now he decided to try and reschedule it, and was glad that Lindsay was able to pull the event together just a few days later than originally planned. Jude now had five days to figure out how to make this silo session better than the last one.

WHERE YOU'D LEAST EXPECT IT

Jude and Theresa decided they would make three trips each day to the hospital to be with the girls. In the morning and at night, they would go together. At noon, Jude would go while Theresa slept, and she would later visit in the afternoon to help with the feedings.

As Jude drove to the hospital for his first solo visit with his little girls, he couldn't stop thinking about his early morning arrival there in the back of the ambulance. Though it had taken place less than a week earlier, it seemed like months had gone by with all that had happened since then.

When he parked his car, instead of going to the birthing center via the normal entrance, Jude decided that he would first stop by the emergency room and thank any nurses or doctors who had been there to help Theresa.

As he walked into the admitting area, the panic that Jude had felt on that frenetic morning a week earlier overwhelmed him. He began recalling the details of that crazy morning.

The calm of the EMTs. The speed of the receiving nurse at the door. The decisiveness of the doctors. The responsiveness of the nurses and staff. Processes were followed, decisions were made, mistakes happened and were corrected immediately.

It was a bizarre and beautiful mix of chaos, coordination, and communication. And it worked.

Suddenly something occurred to Jude. *Most of those people came from different departments.*

And that's when it all clicked.

FLESHING IT OUT

Later that night, after another evening session of watching the girls and saying a tearful good-bye to them, Jude drove his wife and his mother-in-law home and went into his office to work. He knew there was no way he could sleep until he gathered and organized his thoughts around his new theory.

The next morning, as soon as he left the hospital after the first visit of the day, he called Lindsay to run his idea by her. But rather than just blurting it out, he thought he would take a more subtle approach that would test his theory without biasing his client.

"Okay, other than the problem between the nurses and the admissions department, what other groups in the hospital struggle with this silo thing."

Lindsay didn't hesitate. "You name it. Doctors versus nurses. Administration versus doctors. Management versus hourly staff. I think everyone around here sees themselves as members of their own department or clique, more than part of the hospital as a whole."

Jude decided to go fishing. "Is there an example where it's not a problem?" Lindsay didn't respond right away, so Jude baited her just a little. "Are there any departments or places in the hospital where people don't seem to care about what department they're a part of, but work together like a team?"

This time Jude tolerated the silence, giving his client a chance to think it over.

"No." She finally decided.

Jude was disappointed. Until Lindsay continued.

"Other than the ER, I don't think there's a single part of the hospital that—"

Jude interrupted. "What did you just say?"

"I said that I don't think there is anywhere in the hospital that the silo issue isn't a—"

He interrupted her again. "You said other than the ER."

"Well, yeah. But the ER doesn't really count. It's a different animal entirely."

Jude was suddenly excited. "What do you mean?"

"Well, that's the one place in the hospital where there are relatively few departmental issues. But that's true in any hospital, I think. Certainly in the ones where I've worked."

"Why is that, do you think?"

"I don't know," she said, as she pondered the question. "I guess there's no time for it."

Suddenly Lindsay started to back off her answer. "But now that I think about it, I do remember times when there were petty arguments in the ER about budgets and resource sharing."

Jude was determined to salvage his discovery. "You mean doctors and nurses in the emergency room arguing about which department should pay for supplies or equipment?"

"No. Not in the ER itself. I'm talking about during budget sessions and administrative staff meetings."

"Why do you suppose it never happens in the ER itself?" Jude was hoping for a specific answer.

Lindsay paused for a moment. "Because no one with a heart and a brain would even think of bitching about departmental stuff while someone is lying there bleeding right in front of them. Emergencies tend to do that to people."

That was exactly what Jude wanted to hear.

PROCESSING

As the proud and tired parents sat next to their tiny sleeping daughters in the NICU, Jude explained to Theresa his experience in the ER that morning and his conversation with Lindsay.

Though Theresa was not the most focused of audiences—not surprising, given her environment—she made one particularly lucid suggestion. "You should call Brian What's-his-name. The CEO at the fitness machine company."

"Why?" Jude wanted to know.

"Isn't he the guy that said he didn't need your help with the silo thing?"

"Yeah. And I'm finished with my work there."

"Did you ask him why?"

Jude was now just a little impatient. "Yeah, and he said that they just hired a marketing guy and didn't need any help in sales—"

Theresa interrupted her husband. "No, did he tell you why they didn't have a problem with silos? Maybe you can learn something from him."

Jude wanted to argue with her, just to avoid having to say, *"I never really thought of that."* But he couldn't. "You know, that's probably a great idea. I hate when you do that."

They laughed quietly and turned their attention back to Emily and Hailey.

SECOND LOOK

Brian was in his office when Jude called.

"Hey there, Jude. What's new?"

"Not much." Jude said reflexively. And then, catching himself, he explained, "What am I saying? Actually, my whole world is new. Theresa gave birth to our twin girls four days ago."

"I thought she wasn't due for another couple of months." Brian seemed genuinely concerned. "Is everything okay?"

"Yeah, the babies are fine, although they'll be in the hospital for at least three weeks. They need to get their lungs stronger and get bigger. But everything looks good."

"Well, thank God. I appreciate your calling to let me know."

Jude hesitated. "The reason I'm calling is actually about work."

Brian laughed. "I can't believe you have time to work right now. What does your wife think about that?"

"She's fine. Her mom's here and we're doing shift visits to the hospital. Not much else we can do right now. Anyway, I'd like to come by and see you tomorrow for a few minutes. I want to run something by you."

"Let me see." There was a pause. "Yeah, it looks like I'm open tomorrow before nine o'clock, and then from noon to three."

"How about if I come by at noon?"

"Great. Oh, by the way. Where did your wife have the babies?"

"At the hospital."

Brian laughed. "Yeah, I figured that. You must be tired. I mean which hospital."

Jude laughed too. "Oh. John Muir in Walnut Creek. And yeah, I'm exhausted."

"Has she checked out yet?"

Jude thought it was a funny question, but didn't hesitate to answer. "Yeah. She's home."

"Good. Well, both of you get some rest. I'll see you tomorrow."

Jude was looking forward to it.

SCHOOL

Jude arrived at Brian's office the next afternoon, thanked him for the beautiful arrangement of flowers that he had sent to Theresa that morning, and dove right in. He decided to be as direct as possible.

"Okay, I want to know why it is that you don't think you have a silo problem around here."

"It sounds like you're not sure I'm telling the truth." Brian smiled.

Jude was a little embarrassed and backpedaled a bit. "No, that's not what I meant. But do you think it's possible that there is more infighting down there," he motioned to the window overlooking the factory floor below, "than you're aware of?"

"No I don't. But if I'm wrong, I'd like to know so I can fix it." Brian paused for a moment, then dropped his open hand firmly on the desk. "I'll tell you what. Why don't you go down there and find out for yourself?"

Jude was a little puzzled. "What do you mean?"

"I mean go down there and talk to people. Ask them what they think. Talk to anyone in any part of the organization. Most of them know who you are, so they won't be bothered by it. And feel free to ask them in a way that they won't know what you're looking for. I don't want them sugar-coating their answers."

"Are you sure?" Jude was a little hesitant.

"Yeah. Why not? I don't think you'll find anything, but I'd like you to try. Heck, I'll even pay you your hourly rate."

Jude shook his head and laughed. "No, you don't have to do that. But I'll definitely take you up on your offer."

"Okay then. Come back in two hours and let me know what you learn."

Jude checked his watch, and headed for the door. "See you at two o'clock."

SNOOPING

Jude felt like a plainclothes police officer as he roamed the company's halls and factory floor asking questions.

Deciding that it would be best not to bias the people he interviewed, Jude always asked the same two open-ended questions first: "What's going on that's good? What's going on that's not so good?"

While it was certainly true that a few of the more junior people seemed less than comfortable telling a relative stranger anything meaningful about the company, most of the people that Jude talked to were happy to indulge him. And not just on the positive side of things.

Some complained about the budget being too tight. Others thought that the plant needed expanding. Still others wanted to reduce the number of products being manufactured. All in all, however, Jude confirmed what he already knew: Brian ran a pretty tight ship.

Only when people had finished responding to the second question did Jude begin to probe in a more direct way.

He might ask a factory floor worker, "How do you like working with people from finance?" Or he'd ask someone in sales, "Do you think that marketing is doing enough to help you sell products?" He got nothing that would indicate a silo problem.

Jude then began asking a host of more direct, somewhat desperate questions that he thought might elicit some indication of departmental stress. "Which department do you dread working with the most?" "If you had to take resources from one department within the company, which would it be?" Most of those questions provoked looks of confusion more than anything else.

After more than ninety minutes, Jude decided to stop. He went back to Brian's office with a sense of disappointment and admiration. "Okay, I give up."

Brian teased him. "But you've still got a half hour. Maybe you missed something."

"No. I just want to know the answer."

"What answer?"

"How you do it. What's the secret?"

Then Brian said something that Jude didn't want to hear. "I don't know."

"Come on," prodded Jude. "Just tell me."

Brian smiled. "I'm serious. I don't know. It's just how it is." He seemed to be searching for an answer on the ceiling. Then he looked directly at Jude. "Hey, I've got an idea."

Before Jude could ask him, Brian explained. "Why don't *you* try to figure it out? I mean, I'll let you hang around for a while and observe things. I'd like to know why we're different from other companies so we can make sure that we keep doing whatever we're doing."

Normally Jude wouldn't have been so enthusiastic about taking on an unpaid project, but he thought this might be exactly what he needed.

He was right.

CLUE

Jude spent the next three days driving back and forth between his home, the hospital, and the JMJ facility in Manteca, which gave him plenty of time to think.

During those three days, he observed two executive meetings, one focused on operations and another more strategic in nature. He also spent three hours on the factory floor where he watched people work, paying special attention to the various departments represented there. He even went to the parking lot to see when people arrived, who they went to lunch with, who stayed late, and where they parked.

Then one day while he was in the break room getting coffee, he found a brochure of sorts that provided the breakthrough he was looking for. It was a brief history of JMJ, from its founding twelve years earlier to the present.

Thumbing through the booklet, Jude found a chart depicting the company's annual revenue and profit. The trend was moderately positive for the first eight years, until the following period when revenue was cut in half, and profits dropped even more drastically. One year later, both indicators had jumped, and the trend for the following three years since then was nothing short of amazing.

Jude couldn't find any mention of the downturn, so he went to see Brian. Unfortunately, the CEO was already gone, so Jude had to wait another day to have his questions answered.

HISTORY LESSON

After his morning visit to the hospital, where his daughters were already showing signs of progress, Jude went straight to Brian's office.

"Have you figured it out yet?" Brian genuinely seemed to be hoping that he had.

"Not yet," Jude replied, "but I have a few questions for you."

Brian laughed. "This is starting to sound like an episode of *Columbo.* Ask away."

"What happened to the company four years ago?"

"You mean the crisis?"

Jude was confused.

"You don't know about that?" Brian was surprised.

Jude shook his head.

"Wow. I guess it still seems like it happened just yesterday, and that everyone knows about it."

Brian went on to describe what everyone at JMJ had come to refer to as "the Fire Drill."

"A health club in Los Angeles had purchased fifteen treadmills from us," he said, "and one of its customers, a minor celebrity, had a serious accident while using one of them. The story hit the press, the health club blamed us, competitors took advantage of the situation, and our lawyers gave us the horrible advice to avoid making any public statements that might hurt us in court.

"Within a week, customers began canceling orders and returning recently purchased equipment. Sales dried up, and we were staring at a major layoff, and possibly a shutdown within six months."

And that's when Brian made the most enlightening comment of all. "You know, sometimes I think that was the best thing that ever happened to this company."

PUZZLE PIECES

Jude thought he might be able to predict what Brian was going to say next, but he wanted to hear it straight from his ex-client just to make sure he wasn't imagining things.

"I pulled my team together in the boardroom and told them that we had six weeks to restore our reputation. That meant we had to demonstrate that our products were safe, to rebuild our reputation in the market, to fix our relationships with key customers, and to rebuild morale down there." He pointed to the manufacturing floor. "And we had to avoid a nasty lawsuit with that game show host."

"And?" Jude wanted to know what happened.

"Well, we sent two of our techs down to LA and found out that the health club had installed the machines incorrectly. That was no surprise, because we knew the equipment was safe. And then we took a risk that our lawyers didn't like. We ran full-page ads in the four biggest trade publications, telling the whole story. We sent copies of those ads, blown up to three times their normal size, to every person that we had ever had contact with at every client that had purchased one of our machines over the previous five years."

Jude's eyes went wide.

Brian laughed. "Pretty crazy, huh? But you know whose idea that was?" He didn't wait for Jude to answer. "One of our quality control technicians. A twenty-two-year-old young lady. Heck, we decided that the only way to salvage morale was to get everyone involved, even a little pissed off, about what had happened to us. They came up with ideas that none of us up here would have had the courage for."

"I guess you won the lawsuit then." It was a question.

"No, we settled it. For something like twenty thousand dollars."

Jude was confused. "But I thought it wasn't your fault."

"It wasn't. But we would have wasted so much time and money fighting it. I know it's wrong, but unfortunately that's how the legal system works these days, especially in California. But we didn't really care at that point, because we were so busy handling the increase in orders that had already started to come in just a few weeks after the ads went out. Heck, we even decided to pay the settlement for the dopey health club in LA when they agreed to buy their next twenty-five machines from us."

Jude was now starting to get excited. "Tell me the truth, Brian. Before all that happened, was there a silo problem around here?"

Brian thought about it. "Well, I once had to fire a few department heads because they didn't seem to care as much about the company as they did about their own little fiefdoms. If that's what you mean, then I suppose we had some of that."

"What about before you arrived?"

Brian nodded. "Yeah, I remember hearing about a time when the executive offices and marketing departments were located in a different building from the factory because the head of marketing thought his people should have a more 'professional' work environment. And before I came, the incentive trips were limited to people in the sales organization, but I made it a company-wide thing. Some of the salespeople weren't too happy about that at first."

"And since then? Any of that kind of stuff ever pop up?"

Brian thought hard. "Not really. Except maybe when things are going too smoothly. That's probably when I see people start to turn inward a little. But ever since the Fire Drill, we're pretty much together."

Jude thanked Brian and headed for the door.

"So I guess you're thinking that the Fire Drill had something to do with us not having a silo problem."

Jude smiled. "I'll get back to you on that."

CRAMMING

Jude was convinced that the next two weeks would determine the fate of his consulting career. During that time he would try to distill everything he had learned from Brian into an actionable solution and design an effective session for Children's Hospital. If that went well, he'd go back to the Madison for a second try, and then be ready for Carter Bell at Batch.

That was the plan, anyway. But as Jude was learning more and more every day, things don't always go as planned.

OPPORTUNITY CALLS

Just as he pulled his car into the parking lot at the hospital for his evening visit with the twins, the phone rang. Jude recognized the area code and prefix as a Batch number.

It was Carter Bell's assistant.

"Hello Jude, I'm calling for Carter. His trip has changed, and so he won't be able to meet with you next week."

Before Jude could get too disappointed, she added, "But he could fit you in tomorrow at nine o'clock."

Without really thinking about what he was saying, Jude responded, "That would be great."

"Okay, we'll see you at nine tomorrow." And she hung up.

Before he knew what had happened, Jude had an entirely new dilemma on his hands. *What am I going to do now?*

ONWARD

As he sat down next to his wife to watch their babies, Jude explained what had just happened on the phone.

As usual, Theresa reassured her husband. "Listen, there's no way that you could have turned down that appointment. Who knows how long it would have been before you could get back on his calendar?"

Jude agreed, and decided it was time to stop thinking about work and focus on his daughters. These visits usually had a dual impact on Jude.

On one hand, they calmed him by putting life in perspective and helping him realize that his business issues were not as important as he might make them out to be. On the other hand, they reminded him of his financial responsibilities to his family. As usual, the effects canceled each other, leaving Jude to go home no more nor less stressed than when he went in.

At midnight, Jude was still trying to figure out exactly what he would say at Batch the next day, and by 5 A.M.

he decided that it was either coming together or he had lost his ability to assess the quality of what he was doing. Whatever the case, he had to wrap it up so he could grab a shower, get to the hospital, and be over at Carter's office by nine.

Though he was tired and not completely confident of what he was about to cover, he took some consolation from the fact that he certainly knew Carter's business, and the nature of the Batch organization. That would prove to be more important than even Jude could have imagined.

CARTER

Entering the Batch offices for the first time since leaving the company didn't feel as strange to Jude as he thought it would. But then again, he was coming back to meet with the CEO. Unfortunately, whatever friendly vibes Jude had felt from him on the phone seemed to have disappeared by the time the meeting began.

"So, what did you want to talk to me about?" Those were the first words out of Carter's mouth when Jude sat down in the leather chair across the desk. And before he could respond, Carter continued. "I've got just fifteen minutes before my next meeting."

Jude did his best not to seem flustered by the tone of the conversation, or by the shortened time period that he would have to work with. In fact, he decided that he would have to abandon whatever fears he had, and get right to the point.

"Here's the deal. I think Batch has a huge silo problem, and that it's costing you in many ways. I just don't see you turning things around until you eliminate the departmental politics that exist. People are so internally focused that customers are being ignored, and competitors are having their way with you."

Carter was quick to respond. "I am so tired of hearing about that. Everyone thinks that—"

Some combination of exhaustion and courage prompted Jude to interrupt his former CEO. "Listen, if you think I'm making this up, all you need to do is talk to the people two levels below—"

Carter cut him off. "Making it up? What are you talking about? I'm not in denial here. This problem is everywhere."

Jude was relieved, and wasn't quite sure how to redirect his passion. Luckily, Carter continued.

"It's been almost a full year since the announcement of the merger, and I'm still hearing people talk about Hatch Systems and Bell Technology. You'd think that with the stock in the toilet people would stop caring about their old company and focus on making the new one work."

Jude waited until he was finished before diving in. "I'm a little surprised. I figured by now that the Bell and Hatch problem would be less of an issue. If anything, I'd have expected you'd have new silos altogether."

"Are you kidding? Have you forgotten about the advertising crap that went on? Heck, people are still complaining about me not giving enough responsibility to ex-Hatch people, or vice versa."

Jude was starting to feel that Carter was confiding in him, so he pushed a little. "So this is among your staff members too?"

After a brief pause, Carter nodded his head. "Yeah. Which is why I've replaced about half of them in the past three months."

This was a surprise to Jude, who had found it too painful to follow any news about the company after abandoning his hopes of a rebound.

"How has that worked out?" Jude asked, trying to disguise the fact that it was the first he had heard of it.

Carter thought about it. "Well, I definitely swapped out the right people. And I've finally cut my staff down to a manageable size."

"How are they working together so far?"

"Well, we brought in a guy to do team building, to help us become more of a, well, a team, I guess."

"How was it?" Jude asked, expecting the worst.

"The guy was great, actually. At least that's what I thought at the time. I felt like we made a bunch of progress, and everyone else did too. No one bitched about it at all and I would have sworn that we're as tight as any team I've ever worked with. No more passive-aggressive B.S., and almost none of that back-channel gossip that you probably dealt with when you were here."

"So what went wrong?"

Carter shrugged. "I don't know. In spite of all the improvement we made as a team, the silo stuff is still there.

People in marketing are still complaining about engineering. And sales thinks marketing isn't doing enough to move products. The list goes on and on."

"And you're sure that people on your staff aren't just hiding the personal politics better?"

Carter thought about it, and then nodded emphatically. "Yeah. These people genuinely like each other, and they don't hold anything back. That's something I'm good at sensing. This isn't a petty group of people anymore. They really want to succeed, and they don't care who gets the credit."

"You're sure about that?" Jude had to know.

"Yes, I'm sure. Why? You don't believe me?" Carter seemed just a little agitated now.

Jude didn't want to lose him. "No, no. It's not that. I think you probably know what's going on. It's just that if what you're saying is true, then I think I might know how to help you."

Carter now seemed to shift his attention away from his own problem and toward assessing the consultant sitting in front of him.

Jude continued, feeling a new surge of confidence, which mixed nicely with his desperation. "In fact, I'm pretty confident that I can."

He could sense that Carter believed him, and appreciated his directness. The sales call was almost over and an exhausted Jude was ready to get out of there. In minutes, he could be out the door with another paying client on the books.

And then the phone rang. Carter picked it up and spent the next two minutes in a fairly intense conversation. When he hung up, he turned to Jude. "Okay, it's time for my meeting. What does your day look like today?"

Jude was a little taken aback. "Well, at noon I've got to be at—"

Carter jumped in. "Nothing till noon?"

Jude shook his head.

"Good. Come with me."

Before he knew what was happening, Jude was following Carter Bell across the hall and into the boardroom, where the executive team was waiting. There were just seven of them, three of whom Jude had never seen.

Trying to appear as confident as a sleep-deprived man can, Jude couldn't help but think to himself, *What have I gotten myself into?*

REAL TIME

Carter wasted no time. "Okay, everyone. I know we're supposed to be talking about our budget today, but I'm going to mix things up a little bit."

He turned to Jude, who was now seated at the end of the table near the white board. "You all remember Jude Cousins, who ran advertising and other related programs for us when Zachary was still head of marketing. He's going to spend a half hour helping us figure out how to get rid of these damn silos that I've been complaining about for the past six months."

The CFO spoke first. "Does this mean we're not going to be doing the budget today, because my people have been working for the past three nights to—"

Carter interrupted. "Frankly, Dan, I don't know if we're going to get to the budget. And please don't take this wrong, but I wish you'd stop referring to them as *your people*." He turned to one of the other executives. "Or your people. Or yours."

The room was a little stunned by the direct but gentle reprimand, which continued. "I mean, they're *our* people, and we have got to stop thinking about our departments all the time, and which one gets more money and head-count and. . . . "

He didn't seem to know how to finish the sentence. Turning back to Dan, he said, "And besides, what use is the budget conversation if everyone's just going to be lobbying for their departments? I mean, Jude is right."

Jude wanted to stop the rambling CEO right there, but it was too late.

"We aren't going to turn this thing around as long as we keep working in these silos. And you know, it's not our employees' fault. It's ours."

The head of sales, whom Jude knew fairly well from his days at Batch, raised his hand but didn't wait to be called upon. Smiling at Jude with a look of mild surprise, he asked, "Did you say that?"

Before Jude could respond, Carter answered. "No, I did."

The sales VP turned his attention to the CEO. "Come on, Carter. We've come a long way in the last few months. I honestly think we've eliminated most of the stuff that people used to pull in terms of pointing fingers and talking behind everyone's backs."

One or two others nodded their agreement.

Until the head of engineering spoke. "Then why aren't we making any progress? And why are our people still so frustrated with each other?"

Carter held up his hand to put an end to the discussion. "And that is exactly what we're going to talk about today."

The room was suddenly quiet. Carter looked toward Jude and sat down. All attention shifted toward the former employee from marketing.

BLIND PASSION

Jude stood and went to the white board, not knowing exactly how to begin. He decided to start with a question.

"Has anyone here ever worked for a company in crisis?"

After an awkward pause, the head of sales spoke up, smiling. "Well, I'd say this isn't exactly a picnic we're in the middle of here."

The room laughed hard at the gallows humor. Except Carter.

Jude continued. "No, I mean a real crisis. A 'ship-is-about-to-go-down' kind of crisis."

Another moment of silence, broken finally by the CFO. "I was part of an organization once where everyone was pretty convinced the ship was about to go down."

Jude prodded him. "What was the situation?"

With a straight face, he explained. "I was in the Navy in Vietnam. Our boat hit a small mine and was about to go down."

The room broke out into laughter again. Even Carter.

Jude laughed with them and pushed on. "Okay, how about a business example?"

Now that the room had lightened up a bit, the answers were more forthcoming.

The head of sales raised his hand. "Years ago I worked for a kitchen appliance manufacturer in the Midwest. We sold a ton of ovens and stoves. And then trade policies changed and foreign manufacturers with cheaper labor started introducing less expensive models, and our market share tanked."

"Okay. What did you do?"

"Well, at first we sulked, and then we talked about trying to reduce our costs. But we quickly realized that there was no way we could compete on price."

Jude noticed that the other executives seemed genuinely interested in this classic business case. He didn't want to lose them. "Keep going."

"So we decided we had to reposition our brand and our company for the high-end, premium market where we could protect our margins. And we had to do it in less than a year, or we would be toast."

"And?"

"Well, I'm sure some of you have a DeWitt stove or oven in your homes right now."

Many of them nodded, impressed by the personal connection to the story.

"We transformed that company in six months."

Jude was ready to take over the lesson again, glad to be feeling less anxiety than when he started. "Okay, why do you think you were able to do that? I mean, most companies I know wouldn't be able to reposition like that in six *years*."

The sales VP responded without hesitation. "We didn't have a choice."

"Exactly." Jude was coming alive. "It was a crisis. A rallying cry. A crisis brings out the best in companies."

The CFO chimed in. "That's true. When I look back at my career, the best work we did was usually when our backs were up against the wall."

Now Carter had a question. "So are you suggesting that we create a crisis?"

Jude paused, as if he were considering the question. "Well, if that's the only way to rally people, then yeah."

The room was surprised by the answer, and Jude could feel their respect for him slipping away. Which was what he wanted.

"But I don't think that's the smartest way to do it."

Carter seemed relieved.

Jude continued. "I think a company should find a way to rally people around a common cause *before* a crisis hits."

Now he had their attention and was about to move forward. Until the chief legal counsel spoke up. "You know," she said, "every crisis doesn't lead to nirvana. Sometimes the ship really does sink. I've worked at two companies where crises tore the place apart."

Jude was starting to feel like he was in a boxing match, caught with a surprise punch from an opponent he was about to knock out. He paused, trying to collect his thoughts.

And then it occurred to him. "That's right. A crisis has as much power to tear an organization apart, even create thicker silos, as it does to tear the silos down and unite people. It depends on what the executive team does with it."

"What does that mean?" Carter wanted to know.

Jude turned to the head of sales. "Well, what did you guys do at the appliance company?"

"What do you mean?"

"I mean, how did you turn the company around?" Jude couldn't believe he was standing in the boardroom at his old company, grilling one of the executives who had inadvertently caused him to quit his job eight months before. *What a difference it makes to be an outsider,* he thought to himself.

The sales VP thought about the question. "I don't know. We did a lot of things."

Jude was patient. "Yeah, but what were the big things?"

After a long three seconds, the VP explained. "Well, I guess the first thing we talked about was redesigning the products, especially the look and feel and operating features. And we had to rebrand the company to reflect the new market we were going after. A new logo, new collateral, different advertising."

Jude was learning on the fly now. Instinctively, he went to the white board and wrote "Redesign the Product" and "Rebrand the company."

"Go on," he politely urged his former colleague.

"Well, we had to reprice everything too. And then do a big campaign with our distributors and wholesalers who would be representing us in stores. That was huge."

Now Jude wrote "Repricing" and "Distributor Education."

The VP of sales was now staring at the white board, thinking about the situation. "Oh yeah. We had to teach our employees to think about and talk about our business differently. We did a massive retraining."

After Jude wrote "Retraining" on the board, he asked, "Anything else?"

"Well, yeah, there were hundreds of other things we did. But those are the biggies. I think everything else fell into one of those categories. In fact, now that you've got me thinking about it, we had a list that looked something like that, and we used it as our agenda at every meeting for almost a year. I think there were about eight or nine things on it, but I can't remember what else."

Things were starting to click for Jude now. He could feel his adrenaline pumping. "So what about you?" He asked the team, more loudly than he had intended. "What would this look like for Batch?"

Carter smiled, almost laughing at the enthusiastic young consultant. "Whoa, Trigger. What are you talking about?"

The others laughed too. Even Jude smiled, surprised by his own exuberance. "Well, I'm thinking that there's no reason for you not to have a short list of major topics like this. I mean, pretend there's a crisis."

The executives in the room were caught somewhere between skepticism and buy-in, neither pushing for or against what Jude was saying.

Then Carter stood up and went to the board, prompting Jude to take the CEO's seat, which was the only empty one at the table.

"I have an idea. What was the rallying cry for you guys at DeWitt?" he asked, looking at the sales VP.

"Survival." He said, laughing. "Survival through repositioning."

Carter wrote the phrase on the white board above the other five. "So, all of this other stuff is how you defined survival, then?" It was both a question and a statement.

"Right."

"Without that rallying cry, though, it would have been impossible to know what the five building blocks were. Right?"

Now everyone nodded.

"So what is our rallying cry?" After a pause, he continued. "That's not a rhetorical question. I want everyone to take a stab at this right now. If DeWitt had to survive by repositioning, what is it we should be focused on."

Jude could not have been happier. Carter was not only getting it, but he was even helping Jude figure it out.

The CEO walked over to Jude and handed him the marker. "You take over, boss. I want to think about this."

Jude went to the board while Carter resumed his seat.

After a full two minutes, Jude could see the writing coming to an end, so he called the question. "Okay, what do we have?"

The CFO went first. "I think we have to rationalize our expenses and eliminate redundancy."

Jude wrote it on the board, then turned and pointed to the head of engineering.

"I think we need to eliminate unprofitable products and focus on the ones we think have a future."

Jude captured it and turned to the head of sales. "I want to figure out what our new value proposition is, and get our messaging clear."

Next was the head of marketing. "I agree with that. Honing our message is critical."

The VP of customer service agreed with her colleague in engineering and supported the product cleanup, while the legal counsel went with expense reduction and rationalization.

Finally, Carter weighed in. "I like all of those. And I'd add something about staffing. I think we have some key positions to fill, and some poor performers and cultural misfits deeper in the organization to deal with."

When Jude finished writing, he addressed Carter, who looked puzzled. "What's wrong?"

"What do you mean?" The CEO seemed surprised by the question.

"You're frowning."

Carter smiled, not realizing that his facial expression was giving away this thoughts. "I don't know. I guess I was hoping that there would be one big, clear thing."

Everyone in the room was staring at the white board now.

And then Jude saw it. The ideas everyone had been proposing were actually the building blocks. The rallying cry itself was something different.

"I think I see it." He said calmly. Going to the white board, he drew a box above the answers that he had just recorded there. "All of the things you've been saying are the building blocks. The rallying cry itself is something like this." In the box he wrote, "Complete the merger and launch the new company."

Stepping back he waited for a reaction. It came from the CFO. "I think that's it."

No one else said anything for a few long seconds.

Then Carter said, "Yep. That's what we have to do."

The others all started to nod, and Jude felt that they were not merely agreeing with their CEO but buying in to the validity of the answer.

Then the CFO raised his hand. "What's the time frame here?"

No one responded right away so he clarified the question. "I mean, when should we expect to have this all done?"

"I don't know," Jude replied, genuinely unsure of the right answer and eager to hear what the executives in the room thought. "What makes sense?"

"Isn't there a general rule of thumb about this?" Carter asked. "Like a year?"

Jude frowned. "That's what most companies do. But I don't think there is any real logic behind that other than the typical planning cycle and financial schedule."

He waited to see if anyone would push back, then continued. "I mean, I think the time frame around this stuff should depend on what you think is required, realistic, and meaningful in your industry."

The head of human resources raised her hand and spoke up. "Yeah, in a start-up I was involved in, we thought about things in terms of weeks and months, but when I worked at a university, it was always about a year or more. Things moved much more slowly in academic circles. I think we're probably somewhere in between."

That seemed to make sense to everyone. Carter pushed the group for their thoughts. "So what should ours be? What would be acceptable and realistic, given our business?"

The head of sales jumped in first. "I think we can do this in a month. It's been more than a year since the damn merger was finished anyway."

The CFO countered. "I'd like to agree with you, but the fact is we haven't addressed some of these things at all yet, and it's going to take much longer than that. I say we give ourselves a year."

"A year?!" shot back the sales VP.

Jude polled the room for their thoughts and received a variety of answers, most of them between three and six months. He then looked to Carter. "Okay, there's no right answer here. What's the call?"

Carter thought about it for a quick second, and declared, "Five months. That gives us till the end of the year. If that's a little aggressive, then good."

Everyone in the room nodded assent.

It was clear to Jude that they had all bought in to the time frame, and that his theory made sense. And that's when it dawned on him that he no longer felt tired.

REALITY CHECK

As happy as Jude was that the team was buying in to the concepts that he was just figuring out himself, he decided that he should push them a little further to make sure it would work.

He went to the white board, erased what was already there, and rewrote it all in words that made more sense:

Complete the Merger and Launch the New Company

- Eliminate redundant expenses
- Eliminate redundant products
- Fill key roles/replace cultural misfits
- Refine messaging and value proposition

"So, if we rationalize our expenses, pare down our product line, clarify our messaging to the market, and finish hiring and firing, will we be confident in saying that we have finally put the merger behind us and are now a single new company?"

No one nodded at first. Like Jude, they were studying the chart and thinking.

Jude rephrased the question. "Is there anything that's missing? If all we do during the next five months are these things, will we look back and call it a success?"

Immediately the CFO replied. "No way. We have to make our numbers."

The head of sales agreed. Carter looked at Jude as if to say *yeah, what about the numbers?*

Jude was momentarily shaken. Before he could respond, the chief legal counsel chimed in. "Yeah, and we have to deal with the two lawsuits we talked about last week."

The human resources VP added, "And we've got performance reviews to do, and management training."

Jude felt as though the validity of what they had been working on so far was crashing right in front of him. *How could we have missed all of these critical activities?* As hard as he tried, he couldn't figure out how to fit them in with the rallying cry.

Fortunately, Carter bailed him out. "Wait a second. All of that is what we do for a living."

People seemed confused so the CEO continued. "Those are the things that we'll always be doing. We'll always have to make our numbers, and deal with lawsuits, and do annual performance reviews and training. And for that matter, advertising, accounting, product development, and company picnics."

Jude finally figured it out too. "So those are the ongoing operating requirements. But this other stuff," he motioned to what he had written on the board, "is unique to this five-month period, because after that, it either goes away or becomes standard."

Carter added to Jude's explanation. "And sure, if we don't do the ongoing stuff, none of this matters. But if all we do is focus on that, we never really make any progress as an organization."

Slowly, one by one, the executives seemed to be getting it. But more obstacles were yet to be discovered.

TEAM NUMBER ONE

Just as the team seemed ready to finalize the model on the board, the legal counsel raised her hand. "I still don't understand where I fit into this. I mean, none of that stuff up there falls under my area of responsibility."

The room was quiet as they pondered her question. The head of human resources wanted to make her feel included. "Sure you do. We'll need legal help around the messaging. And I'm going to need your help dealing with difficult employee terminations."

That seemed to mildly placate the chief lawyer. Then Carter jumped in. "Wait a second. I don't think I like your question." There was a slight hint of annoyance in his voice.

Everyone looked at Carter, confused.

"This is not about figuring out how to accommodate all our functional areas. I really don't care about your departments or titles or functional responsibilities. I want all of us focused on what's important, regardless of where it falls in the organization."

He looked at the legal counsel. "And that means I want you, as a member of this team, to be just as involved and interested in what we're doing around products and marketing as you are around legal issues. That's why I put you on my staff. Not because you're a good lawyer, but because you can contribute across the board."

Jude wished he were recording the session, but decided there was no way he would forget this. He added to Carter's explanation.

"And the next rallying cry might have a distinctly legal component, but that won't mean that everyone else in the room won't be involved."

The head of engineering made a rare comment, but an insightful one. "It's almost like we need to disregard our titles when we're together, and then put our functional hats back on when we go back to work."

Everyone was nodding in an "ah ha" kind of way.

"Where did *that* come from?" the CFO teased.

As everyone laughed at the joke, Carter looked at Jude and nodded his head. "This is good."

Jude had never enjoyed being a consultant more than in that moment. Now all he had to do is figure out how to make a living at it.

BACK TO EARTH

Carter decided it was time to get back to the regular agenda, and thanked Jude for his help. The team graciously joined in with a quiet chorus of "nice job" and "this has been really helpful" and even "good to see you again."

As the CEO walked him to the door, he said, "I'll be out of town for about five days starting tomorrow. When I get back, let's talk about what I need to do to make all of this stick."

Jude agreed, said good-bye, and left. He hoped that Carter would be open to bringing him on board as a paid consultant, and not merely content to have picked his brain for an idea. Determined to ride the emotional high from the meeting, Jude rededicated himself to having a great session at Children's Hospital the next day, and even trying to get his foot back in the door at the Madison.

But first, he needed to see his girls. After forty-five minutes of gazing at his daughters, Jude explained the day's events to his wife. She then reminded him of their wager.

"So, I think I'll take my fifty dollars in the form of a nice dinner. How about Lark Creek?"

He agreed. During dinner they talked mostly about the progress their daughters were making and when they would most likely be coming home. But for a few minutes Theresa indulged her husband's need to get his mind around the next steps in his company.

Jude had figured out that he would need three clients paying him on a regular basis to sustain the business. And if he could find a project here and there to supplement that, and then gradually raise his fees, the business would be in good shape by the end of the year.

Theresa wasn't worried. Jude attributed this to her focus on the girls and her unbridled optimism about her husband's abilities. Unfortunately, he wasn't as confident as she was, and he knew that without Children's Hospital, the number of regularly paying clients in his stable would currently be zero.

PART FOUR

Moments of Truth

TEST NUMBER ONE

Jude spent much of that evening preparing for the next morning's session with Lindsay and her team. By the time he arrived in the conference room at the hospital, he was feeling pretty confident that his theory was more solid than ever. But that confidence was offset by the reality that a new group of executives could change everything.

As soon as the team of eight was seated around the table, Lindsay introduced Jude and succinctly explained the reason he was there. "We need to start working as a hospital, and not as separate departments that happen to share a building."

Everyone seemed to be in agreement with the goal.

Jude then went to the front of the room and asked the group a series of questions about their behavior as a team. How comfortable were they in being open with one another? How much did they engage in honest debate? That kind of thing.

After an awkward few minutes, the team opened up. Soon enough Jude came to the conclusion, as Lindsay had suggested he would, that there were no blatant personality clashes among the group and that the silo issue was probably more structural and organizational than interpersonal. So Jude moved to his pitch.

First, he asked them for examples of crisis situations they had been in, and for the next ten minutes helped them come to the realization that teams often perform at their best when their backs are up against a wall.

He told the group about his wife's emergency room experience, which not only was helpful in driving the point home, but seemed to help them come to know Jude as a person rather than just a consultant.

As the lesson was beginning to take hold, out of nowhere Jude asked a rhetorical question of the group, one he decided should be a staple of his workshops in the future: "Why wait for a crisis?"

It was as though he had just told them about electricity.

He continued, with more enthusiasm than he had yet demonstrated to a group of clients. "Why not create the same kind of momentum and clarity and sense of shared purpose that you'd have if you were on the verge of going out of business?"

That set off an outbreak of nods and raised eyebrows from the suddenly engaged audience. Now that he had them where he wanted them, Jude decided to get right to the meat of his session and asked the $64,000 question: "What is the single most important accomplishment that this team needs to make in the next six or nine months?"

The chief medical officer, who oversaw all doctors in the hospital, responded first. "That depends on who you ask. The nursing department is going to have a different answer than administration or marketing."

Lindsay looked at Jude as if to say *and that is exactly the problem*.

Jude was happy to be able to address the issue right away. "Okay, I understand that every department has different areas of focus and expertise. Which is a good thing. But what is it that you need to be focused on for the good of the entire organization? Regardless of your departmental role."

Nothing. It was as though the question had been asked in a different language.

Jude tried another approach. "How about this? Take off your functional hats and think about yourselves as generic leaders without ties to any one department. If I were to come back here next year, what is the most important thing that you would want to be different about the hospital?"

That seemed to spark a few ideas in the minds of the executives.

The chief nursing officer went first. "I'd like to see morale improved. If we don't have a more motivated workforce, I don't see how we're going to be able to sustain the levels of care that we need. And we don't want any union problems like they had in Stockton."

No one seemed to disagree, but the chief medical officer countered, "Don't get me wrong. I'd love to increase productivity and morale too." No one was quite sure that he meant it. "But frankly, I'd rather see us invest in our clinical technology. If we fall behind in that area, none of the rest of this matters."

The chief nursing officer rolled her eyes while the chief operating officer, a small man wearing a bow tie, spoke for the first time that day. "Listen, if we don't fix the infrastructural problems around here then we're going to lose half my people. Everything from billing to scheduling to e-mail is a mess. But every time the docs say they need a new machine, they get it because we're afraid they'll take their business to another hospital."

Now that it was clear that everyone was firmly entrenched in their own areas, Lindsay was starting to get frustrated.

"Does anyone here still think we don't have a problem with politics?" She snapped.

The chief medical officer took issue. "This isn't about politics. It's about doing what's right for our patients."

"And don't forget our doctors." The nursing head chimed in sarcastically.

"Yes, and our doctors." He politely acknowledged. "Without them, our patients aren't going to be too happy."

"And the nurses don't play a critical role in that?" she asked, calmly.

"Well sure, but even a great nurse can't help a patient who doesn't have the right equipment."

The head of human resources sighed, and then made a declaration. "I am so tired of hearing about whether nurses or doctors are more important! Who cares? We need both. And for that matter, we need accountants and cafeteria workers and janitors, and yes, even human resource administrators."

In a rare moment of comedic solidarity, the doctor and nurse looked at each other as if to say, "Do we really need human resource administrators?"

The HR head started to get a little emotional now. "Listen you guys. Every time one of my people comes to one of yours," she motioned to the heads of doctors and nurses, "and asks them to do something that isn't directly about a patient, they treat them like they're a child. They come back to me completely demoralized, which is ridiculous, because all they're doing is their jobs. If you don't think we're doing the right things in HR, then tell me and we'll take a look at it. But if you don't think we should be doing anything at all, then please, put me out of my misery and fire me so I can go somewhere where people understand the value of good management."

She paused, and everyone thought she was finished. Then another thought seemed to cross her mind and she continued, with even more emotion now. "You know, just because my people didn't go to medical school or cut patients open for a living doesn't mean they don't care about patients. It's just that the way they care about patients is to take care of the people who take care of those patients. It wouldn't hurt us to acknowledge that from time to time."

The last statement hit everyone in the room where it needed to. No one spoke for a long five seconds.

Before the next phase in the turf war could begin, Jude jumped in to redirect the conversation a little. "Okay, I want everyone here to take off the departmental hats you're wearing." Going around the room one by one he explained. "That means you're not a doctor, you're not a nurse, you're not an administrator, you're not an HR person, and you're not a community relations or communications or whatever it is you're in charge of kind of person." They laughed at Jude's inability to remember the external affairs title.

"You're all now wearing a hat that says 'Executive of Children's Hospital of Sacramento.' That's it."

He paused to let it sink in, and then reframed the question for the group. "Which of the things you've described so far, or maybe something you haven't mentioned yet, has to be done in order for the hospital to give itself the best chance of achieving its long-term goals?" He looked down at a piece of paper sitting on the table in front of him. "It says here that your five-year goal is to become the best hospital in Sacramento, and one of the top ten pediatric hospitals in the country. Right?"

They all nodded without hesitation, making it clear to Jude that they were both clear and on board.

"Okay, good." Jude was relieved to have agreement around something. "So what is the biggest impediment to that happening, in terms of the next year or so?"

Everyone was considering the question when the chief operating officer weighed in. "It has to be patient support services. That's our biggest Achilles' heel. I think we're strong in terms of medical technology and quality of doctors and nurses, but we're dropping the ball when it comes to old-fashioned customer service and communication. It's all too confusing and disjointed for patients."

Amazingly, everyone slowly started to nod.

The chief nursing officer went first. "I actually agree with that. I mean, we can always improve in terms of clinical stuff. But it's the hand-offs and follow-up that we stink at. And frankly, we've all seen the surveys. That's what people remember most about their experience, whether they're here for surgery, birthing, or just testing."

The doctor countered. "I'm just uncomfortable taking my eye off of clinical technology."

The head of external affairs jumped in. "Are you wearing your doctor hat or your executive hat?"

Reluctantly, the doc admitted, "Okay, it's my doctor's hat. But I still don't want to—"

Now Lindsay interrupted him. "Listen, we're not going to let this hospital ignore clinical care. But we're going to have to make difficult decisions and trade-offs sometimes. And I'd prefer it if we could figure out those trade-offs together."

After a brief moment of silent consideration, Lindsay declared a temporary answer. "Okay, let's assume that patient service is it. Then what?" The question was directed at Jude.

He wrote "Patient Service" on the board and said, "Everyone write down two or three or four things that we would need to do to turn this situation around."

The head of marketing raised his hand. "So what do you call that?"

Jude didn't seem to understand the question, so the marketing VP clarified. "Is that a goal or an objective, or what is it?"

Jude looked at the white board as though the answer were written on it somewhere. "I don't know. I guess I'd call it a—" he paused, "a theme. Or maybe a thematic goal."

Three of the people wrote down his answer and Jude decided it was probably the right label for what he had been previously referring to as the rallying cry.

Jude continued. "Okay, everyone write down the handful of things that need to happen if we're going to accomplish our thematic goal of improving patient service."

Then the CFO raised his hand. "You want numbers?"

"No. Definitely not. All I'm looking for are big fat categories of things that need to be accomplished. Keep it as general as you can. We'll deal with numbers later."

The executives went to work, completely focused on the exercise now. Jude decided that none of them were evaluating him or what he was doing; they were thinking about the business. Which was all he could ask for at this point.

After three or four minutes, Jude surveyed the room, pointing to each executive for a response. By the time everyone had spoken, Jude had written four different subject areas on the board:

- Better patient throughput
- Integrated clinical information systems
- Improved case management
- More joint planning

As they studied the various areas, Jude asked, "What's missing? If we did everything on this list, what could still cause us to fail in terms of patient satisfaction?"

"Oh wow, we forgot something huge." It was the CFO. "What about outpatient scheduling and communication. Isn't that where we always seem to get dinged?"

He had definitely hit a nerve.

"Yeah, that one will kill us if we don't do something about it soon," added the head doctor, much to everyone's quiet delight.

Jude put it on the list and stood back for a moment to let them soak it all in.

Then he decided not to wait for someone to ask the next inevitable question. "Now, I bet some of you are thinking, *What about our day jobs?* Rest assured that we're not forgetting about the fact that we have to continue doing surgery and treating patients and paying bills and collecting insurance."

The muted laughter and smiles on the faces of some of the executives made it clear that they were indeed thinking the same thing.

"Those tasks are and will always be critical. But if that's all we're thinking about, then every month and every quarter and every year that goes by won't make this a better hospital." Jude made a note to himself to thank Carter for providing some of the language he was using.

"All makes sense to me," declared the head doctor energetically. "This is right on target."

The look on the faces of the people around the table was one of momentary shock. Jude would later learn that the chief medical officer was the team's cynic, someone who rarely acknowledged a good idea that wasn't his own. They couldn't believe he had been so enthusiastic.

DEEPER

"What's next?" asked Lindsay. "I like it too, but it seems like we need more clarity than that."

Jude was glad that she was doing the pushing, and not her staff. He didn't want them to see her as rooting for him.

"The next step is twofold." He pointed to the white board. "First, figure out how to measure each of these areas. And then come up with a short list of ongoing operational objectives that you need to track in addition to this stuff."

"How exactly do we track it?" the COO wanted to know. "Do we need an online tool or something?"

Jude shook his head. "I don't think so. The key is reviewing it during your staff meetings. This should become your scoreboard or your grounding tool for every meeting."

Lindsay frowned, not quite on board yet. Jude could see she wasn't getting it, so he continued his explanation.

"Every time you get together for a meeting, you should start by asking yourselves how you're doing in regard to these areas."

"You mean, we should go through all the metrics?" she wanted to know.

This was new territory for Jude, so he was going with his gut now. "No, I'm thinking that you should keep it more qualitative than that. It seems like when you start with data people's eyes glaze over and you lose them."

The head of marketing agreed. "Either that or they get so wrapped up in the details that they lose sight of the bigger picture."

Lindsay wanted more evidence. "Let's try it right now, without the data, and see how it works."

Jude smiled and turned to the white board. "Why not? Okay, let's use a simple way of evaluating these areas. How about rating them one through five?"

Lindsay shook her head. "No. Even that gets confusing. If we're going to keep it simple, let's keep it real simple. How about green, yellow, and red? Green for 'on track,' yellow for 'not quite there or not quite sure,' and red for 'definitely not where we need to be.'"

Jude was happy to try it. "All right, let's start with the first area. How would we rate our current situation in terms of arrivals and departures?"

For the next ten minutes, the team went through the five topics, reporting their assessments and then trying to arrive at a general consensus around the final color rating for each area:

Better Patient Throughput	yellow
Integrated Clinical Information	red
Improved Case Management	yellow
Joint Planning	yellow
Outpatient Management	red

"Shouldn't at least one category be green?" the CFO wanted to know.

Jude shrugged. "Well, if something is in good shape or on track or ahead of schedule, then yeah, it would be green. And that will probably be the case in some situations. But because we're just starting out, it makes sense that everything is red or yellow."

As the team studied the chart, Jude decided something was missing. "You know, let's go ahead and add the standard operating categories so that we have all the big stuff in front of us."

"Have we decided what those categories are?" Lindsay asked him.

"No, let's do it now. We shouldn't have more than four or five, I would think."

The team then had a fifteen-minute discussion and settled on the following areas for ongoing measurement:

- Occupancy of Beds
- Clinical Outcomes

- Operating Income
- Staffing Ratios
- Cost per Discharge

Jude wrote them on the board and looked back at the original five categories. "Let's see. What should we call these things that define the thematic goal?" He looked to the group for a suggestion.

"I like what you called it before," the head of nursing said. "What was it, *big fat categories of stuff,* or something like that?"

Jude laughed. "Well, maybe we need something just a little more descriptive."

The chief medical officer saw an opportunity to come up with an original thought. "Why don't you call them Defining Objectives? That's what they do, give definition to the thematic goal."

No one objected, and Jude liked it as much as anything he could think of. "Okay, so we've got a thematic goal, defining objectives, and then the standard operating objectives." He looked at the board.

With a sense of passion he challenged the team. "Someone tell me why this shouldn't create the context for every staff meeting you have."

After a pause, they began shaking their heads as if to say *I don't see any reason not to.*

Lindsay spoke next. "Tell us again exactly how this is going to solve our silo problem."

Before Jude could say anything, the CFO jumped in. "Because now if anyone argues for something that's good for their department or functional area but doesn't have a meaningful impact on any of these things," he motioned to the board, "then we'll all be able to explain why it shouldn't be a priority."

The chief nursing officer added, "And to be honest, now that we've clarified this, it would be much harder for me to even think about lobbying for the nurses at the expense of what we're trying to do overall."

"I don't think it's going to be quite that easy." It was the COO, in a tone that was challenging, but not bitter. "When we go back to our areas and get bombarded by our people with what they want and need to do their jobs, I think it will be hard not to go back to the way things were before."

Jude agreed. "You're right. And that's why we need to keep coming back to this."

Lindsay was suddenly fired up, and spoke out with more force than usual. She seemed to be responding to what her COO had just said. "Then let me be very clear to everyone here. You should all go back to your direct reports and tell them what we're focused on here. We need to help them understand what our priorities are, and why we can or can't do some of the things they want."

She paused for a second. "Heck, why can't we announce this to everyone in the hospital?"

Jude thought about it for a moment. "Well, we'd have to do it in a way that made sense." He was trying, unsuccessfully, to find a reason why it wouldn't be a good idea. "But I guess there's no reason not to. It would create the context for everyone to think about doing their jobs a little differently."

"And it would connect them to the rest of the hospital," agreed the head doctor, "instead of just their area."

There was no doubt in Jude's mind that Lindsay and her team were, to a person, excited about what they had just accomplished. The CEO called for a break, and asked the CFO and Jude to stay behind.

REVENUE

When the room was clear, Lindsay spoke first. "Okay, this is really good stuff. But we're going to need help making it stick." She turned to the CFO. "How much can we afford to pay Jude?"

He hemmed a little. "First, I agree that this is great. And it's worth whatever it costs."

Jude could feel the "but" coming.

"But we've still got to get the budget approved, and right now, I'm afraid we only have about half his retainer covered." He turned to Jude. "I'm sorry, but I think that's the best we can do right now."

Feeling the need to be more gracious than his checkbook would have liked, Jude reassured them. "I understand. Timing is everything sometimes."

Lindsay jumped in. "But there is something else I can do. I'm going to call a few of my friends, the CEO of Stockton General and St. Mary's Hospital in Fresno, and tell them about what you've done here. And I know a woman who took over that automobile manufacturing plant in Fremont. And she probably has plenty of budget for this."

The CFO nodded. "A few of my vendors could use your help, if they're willing to admit it. Like Hiett Linens, the company that provides our uniforms and sheets. I can probably arrange for a meeting with them."

It wasn't money, but it was probably more valuable over the long term, so Jude thanked them enthusiastically.

The second half of the session was spent fleshing out the details of each of the defining objectives. Dates, metrics, specific criteria for determining when something would be finished.

At the end of the afternoon, Lindsay thanked Jude and announced that it wouldn't be the last time the team would see him. They actually applauded, which Jude found surprisingly uncomfortable. But he'd take it—and use it as a source of confidence during his next sales call, where he'd need every bit of support he could find.

SHIFTING GEARS

When Jude arrived home that evening he told Theresa about the success he'd had, as well as his temporary financial setback at the hospital. All in all, though, he was happy.

Uncharacteristically, Theresa seemed unable to focus on what he was telling her. Finally, she explained why.

"The girls are making progress faster than the doctors thought they would." Then she started crying, and not in a joyful way.

"That's great! What's wrong?"

"They're going to be coming home more than a week early. In five days." She paused. "I just don't know if I'm going to be able to handle it."

Jude hugged her. "Are you kidding? You're going to do fine. You'll be a natural."

She argued back gently. "I've gotten so used to having those wonderful nurses and doctors taking care of the girls that I'm afraid for them to leave there. I almost wish they'd keep them for another week. Is that terrible for me to say?"

Jude laughed, consolingly. "No. It's not terrible. It's normal. Don't worry. I'll be here to help you."

"But you've got so much to do at work."

"No. When the girls come home, I'm taking two weeks off completely to be here and help with the transition. And we'll have your mom around too. Listen, I've just got to get a couple more clients firmed up by then."

Jude was wondering just how he was going to pull that off, when he looked down at his wife and noticed she had fallen asleep. That's when it dawned on him how tired she must be after almost three solid weeks of uncertainty and intensity. He too was on the verge of exhaustion, but knew that he needed to keep his energy level up for just another five days if he was going to get some momentum before shifting to full-time parenting for a while.

Not that he had any illusions of that being easier. But somehow, at that moment Jude longed for the challenge of all-night feedings and round-the-clock diaper changes. Anything to avoid going back to the Madison.

PRIDE SWALLOWING

Even by the tone in his voice during the initial phone call, Jude could tell that Dante's feeling toward his consultant had changed since that disastrous presentation. He wasn't rude or particularly cold, but he was certainly a little more distant.

Still, he agreed to meet later that day, which would give Jude an opportunity to convince the CEO to give him another shot at his team. It wouldn't be easy.

Dante wasn't ready to have Jude address his staff again. Not quite yet. "Listen, Jude. Maybe it would be better if you just told me what you'd like to do, and I could relay it to the team."

Jude was torn. He knew that if given the chance, he could bring them around. But he also wanted to respect Dante's situation. After all, a consultant shouldn't be a reason for a CEO to risk losing credibility with his team.

So Jude obliged and dove right in.

First, he talked about the power of a crisis, which Dante found very easy to relate to. And when he said "Why wait for a crisis?" he knew he had him hooked.

Then Jude challenged him to think about what his thematic goal would be. Dante threw out a few ideas. Efficiency. Repeat business. Clearer marketing. None of which seemed like the right idea.

Jude encouraged him to think in terms of broader issues. "What do you want to see happen during the next nine months?"

Then it dawned on the CEO. "I want us to regain the momentum that we once had. I don't want us worrying about the competition and reacting to them. I want us to have a plan and to be enthusiastic about it. To go on the offensive." Dante had convinced himself.

Jude then pushed him to think about the defining objectives and the standard operating objectives, but Dante's head was starting to spin a little. Finally, he said, "Okay, let's have you come back tomorrow to take us through this."

Jude should have been ecstatic. He would have his chance at redemption after all. But once he'd accepted the reality that it wasn't going to happen, he'd actually felt relieved to be off the hook and let Dante make the presentation. The resurrected thought of having to stand in front of the Madison staff again was suddenly unwelcome to Jude.

But I'm his consultant, and I guess this is what consulting is all about, he thought to himself as he booked the meeting for the next day.

THE LIONS' DEN

In addition to agreeing to do the meeting, Jude went so far as to suggest to Dante that he not say too much about what they had talked about the day before. He didn't want to bias the group, and he thought it would be better if they learned about the theory from the beginning.

Thankfully, Dante did kick off the meeting by saying, "Jude is back today, and he has some very interesting ideas to go over with us. He's been a helpful member of our advisory board for the last few years, and I think we'd be crazy not to fully utilize him now as a consultant."

Even without mentioning the previous week's debacle, everyone knew what Dante was talking about.

Jude went to the front of the room feeling like a convict standing in front of a parole board. "Okay, I'd like to talk to you about that silo problem again." He swallowed hard. "I still believe that the responsibility for those silos lies in this room." He paused, letting the comment sink in, then continued. "But I think I've figured out exactly how you can address it."

The front office VP didn't even give Jude a chance to go forward. "So you're coming back here to tell us what we're doing wrong again?" She was as bitter now as she had been before, as though no time had passed since the last session.

Jude was conciliatory. "No, I didn't mean it that way, and I'm not saying that you guys are doing something uniquely wrong. And I admit that I made some mistakes last time, but I'm learning. I just want to show you something I've discovered recently that I think most organizations can do to reduce politics and interdepartmental conflict."

She wasn't about to accept his apology. "But you're saying that we're political. What makes you think—"

Dante interrupted. "Hold on a second, Mikey. I'll tell you right now that I do think we're political. Maybe not in the overtly manipulative way that most people assume politics works. But we've certainly got different agendas. I don't know what it was like for you in high tech, but every hotel I've ever run had politics. And now I'm starting to realize we're the only people who can put an end to it."

Mikey was tough. "Yeah, but when someone comes in here and tells me that I'm being political, I just think that—"

Again Mikey was interrupted. But this time by the head of operations. "Come on, you're the most political person here. Everything is about your department and your people.

Whenever anything goes wrong, it's never something that you or your staff did. It's always our fault. Just once I'd like you to admit that you screwed up."

Jude was feeling a strong mix of emotions. First, he felt bad that the session had already drifted out of control. But he also felt a sense of relief that he wasn't the center of controversy for the time being, and that some semblance of truth seemed to be seeping into the room.

Mikey looked as though she was about to explode, and then she just shut down. Nothing. She folded her arms and turned back to Jude as if to say, *Go ahead.* Which he did.

"Okay, I think that the challenge at the hotel is completely avoidable, and that it's not a matter of personalities but just a lack of shared direction."

The looks on the faces of some of Mikey's colleagues seemed to suggest that personality was definitely at play, but Jude had a point to make and didn't want one person's issues to cloud his lesson. So he pushed on with his planned talk.

By now, Jude was pretty comfortable with the silo lecture. He explained *the power of crisis.* He asked the question, *Why wait for a crisis?* He introduced the concept of *the thematic goal* and *the defining objectives* and *the standard operating objectives.*

Oddly enough, everyone seemed to get hooked by different parts of the model. The head of facilities immediately clicked with the crisis analogy. Most of the others were convinced by the thematic goal and the defining objectives. The CFO wasn't quite on board until the standard operating objectives were included. Everyone, with the exception of Mikey, had been won over.

When the session ended, Jude gladly and graciously accepted a little ribbing from Dante's team. "Hey, this was a little better than last time," was how the CFO put it. Jude knew that his standing at the hotel was on firmer ground. More important, he felt strongly that even if Dante didn't extend his retainer, his work might lead to real progress at the hotel, and that it would work in other organizations too.

For the first time since starting his company, Jude felt certain that he would be a consultant for the rest of his career.

LOOSE ENDS

A few days later Carter called to say that his trip had been extended and that he wouldn't be able to meet with Jude for another two weeks. He assured him that he had every intention of following up, and he even mentioned thematic goals by name, which gave Jude confidence that he was serious.

For the next few weeks, Jude stayed home with his wife and baby girls, losing himself in the trials and joys of early parenthood. Admittedly, he checked e-mail between late-night feedings, but he didn't worry about his business. Not that the financial arrangements had been completely ironed out. But Jude knew that his business depended less on his convincing his current clients to sign on for a long-term engagement and more on the effectiveness of his ideas.

Within a month, Jude's client list included Batch Technology, Children's Hospital, the Madison, the automobile plant in Fremont, and another hospital in Fresno. Each of them encountered meaningful though varying degrees of success in eliminating their silos.

Batch had the greatest level of success, propelling the firm back up onto the technology wave that it had caught early on. Carter and his team finally put the merger behind them, and then used the skills they had developed to rapidly acquire and integrate two additional firms. And when occasional signs of territoriality arose, Carter always went back to the thematic goal and the defining objectives to refocus the team on its collective, common interests.

Children's Hospital struggled at first to bring doctors, nurses, and unions together, but with Lindsay's persistence, it would become one of the twenty best pediatric facilities in the country. Eventually, Lindsay would move on and establish a name for herself as a turnaround specialist.

The CEO of the Fremont automobile plant would become Jude's favorite client. Kathryn Petersen was a hardworking executive with a modest background. She had a knack for building teams, and would provide Jude with an education in that area that would prove to be useful in his work with clients, as well as in the consulting firm that he would eventually build.

The Madison overcame its short-term problem with the front desk and housekeeping teams, part of which could be attributed to Dante's firing his difficult head of services. However, his diminishing patience with the day-to-day challenge of managing interpersonal issues would finally lead him to sell the hotel to one of his chain competitors and buy a series of smaller bed-and-breakfast inns in the Napa Valley.

One of Jude's greatest challenges and most rewarding experiences would be his work with Father Ralph at Corpus Christi Church, where he would learn that silos in churches can be particularly difficult to dismantle, but that the clarity of mission there can be a powerful motivator for doing so.

JMJ Fitness continued to be successful under Brian Bailey. From time to time Jude took on a small project there, but more often than not, he felt he was learning more than he was contributing. Nonetheless, the relationship between client and consultant remained strong for many years.

FAST FORWARD

By the one-year anniversary of the founding of Cousins Consulting, Jude's practice was as varied as ever, allowing him to be the generalist he wanted to be. Still, every engagement seemed to involve, in some way, the idea of rallying executives and their employees around a thematic goal and destroying silos.

Jude's business grew rapidly through word of mouth and strong client references. Over the course of the next three years, the firm had grown to seven consultants and two office staff. Jude leased a small office over a bank just three miles from his home, and went home for lunch with Theresa and his three daughters as much as possible.

On the eighth anniversary of the firm's founding, Cousins Consulting had grown to more than fifteen consultants and five staff members handling marketing, finance, and client support. Vertical markets had been established in health care, technology, education, and nonprofits.

And then one day it happened. It was during a staff meeting.

Jude asked for input about how to allocate marketing dollars for the upcoming year. One of his health care specialists responded first. "We think it's about time that we received our fair share of the budget."

Jude frowned. "Excuse me?"

The consultant started to repeat himself. "We think it's—"

Jude interrupted him. "Who is we?"

"Me and Fred. We think that the health care vertical deserves more money this year."

And there it was. The first real silo to sprout at Cousins Consulting. Though he was tempted to dive in and crush it immediately, Jude decided to let it sit there in the open for a moment so he could appreciate it in all its destructive glory.

Then he crushed it.

The Theory

INTRODUCTION TO SILOS

In *The Five Dysfunctions of a Team* I addressed the interpersonal and behavioral issues that prevent groups of people from becoming teams. I strongly believe that building a cohesive leadership team is the first critical step that an organization must take if it is to have the best chance at success.

However, even when leadership teams become behaviorally cohesive, they face another challenge, a more structural one, that often thwarts their efforts and creates unnecessary politics within an organization. What I'm referring to are silos.

Silos are nothing more than the barriers that exist between departments within an organization, causing people who are supposed to be on the same team to work against one another. And whether we call this phenomenon departmental politics, divisional rivalry, or turf warfare, it is one of the most frustrating aspects of life in any sizable organization.

Now, sometimes silos do indeed come about because leaders at the top of an organization have interpersonal problems with one another. But my experience suggests that this is often not the case. In most situations, silos rise up not because of what executives are doing purposefully but rather because of what they are failing to do: provide themselves and their employees with a compelling context for working together.

This notion of context is critical. Without it, employees at all levels—especially executives—easily get lost, moving in different directions, often at cross-purposes.

Even the most well-meaning, intelligent people get distracted and confused amid the endless list of tactical and administrative details that come their way every day. Pulled in many directions without a compass, they pursue seemingly worthwhile agendas under the assumption that their efforts will be in the best interest of the organization as a whole.

But as employees notice their colleagues in other divisions repeatedly moving in different directions, they begin to wonder why they aren't on board. Over time, their confusion turns into disappointment, which eventually becomes resentment—even hostility—toward their supposed teammates. And then the worst thing possible happens—they actually start working against those colleagues on purpose!

This maddening problem exists, to different degrees, in most companies I've encountered. And in too many of those companies leaders who are frustrated by the silo mentality mistakenly attribute it to the immaturity and insecurity of employees who somehow just refuse to get along with one another.

But the fact is, most employees have a profound and genuine interest in working well across divisions. That's because they, more than anyone else, feel the daily pain of departmental politics as they are left to fight bloody, unwinnable battles with their colleagues.

If there is a place where the blame for silos and politics belongs, it is at the top of an organization. Every departmental silo in any company can ultimately be traced back to the leaders of those departments, who have failed to understand the interdependencies that must exist among the executive team, or who have failed to make those interdependencies clear to the people deeper in their own departments.

Thankfully, there is a simple and powerful way for those leaders to create a common sense of purpose, and a context for interdependency: they must establish, for the executive team as well as the rest of the organization, a rallying cry. A thematic goal.

COMPONENTS OF THE MODEL

The model for combating silos—as illustrated in the fable—consists of four components:

- A thematic goal
- A set of defining objectives
- A set of ongoing standard operating objectives
- Metrics

After each component is explained, various examples are provided for better understanding.

THEMATIC GOAL

Definition: a single, qualitative focus that is shared by the entire leadership team—and ultimately, by the entire organization—and that applies for only a specified time period.

To avoid politics and turf battles, executives must establish an unambiguously stated common goal, a single overriding theme that remains the top priority of the entire leadership team for a given period of time (see Figure 1). In turn, this thematic goal serves to align employees up and down the organization and provides an objective tool for resetting direction when things get out of sync.

Before further exploring the exact nature of a thematic goal, it might be helpful to describe what it is *not*.

A thematic goal is not a long-term vision or, as Jim Collins and Jerry Porras refer to it in their terrific book *Built to Last,* a BHAG (big hairy audacious goal). Nor is it a tactical metric or measurable objective.

While it is certainly a good idea for companies to have both a vision to motivate people over the long term and a set of tactical objectives to guide their daily activities—and most do—the thematic goal lies somewhere in between the two, and I believe it may well be even more important. That's because it bridges the two by making the vision more tangible and by giving the tactical objectives more context.

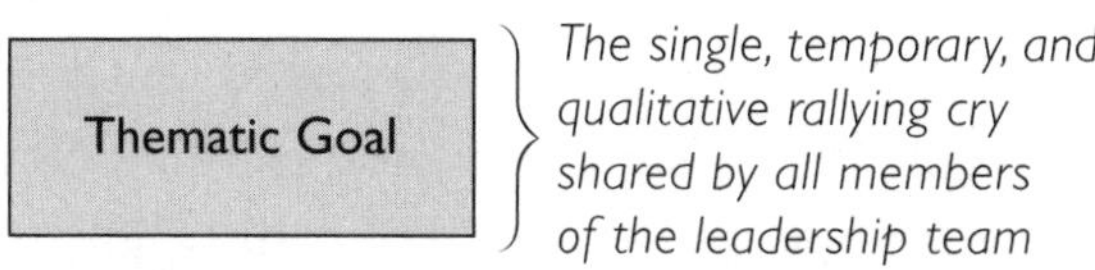

Figure 1. Goal Alignment Structure: Thematic Goal.

Let's look at the key elements of a thematic goal to understand how this happens.

Single

In an organization, there can be only one true thematic goal in a given period. That's not to say there aren't other desires, hopes, and objectives at play, but none of them can be attempted at the expense of accomplishing the thematic goal.

Every organization needs a top priority. When a company is tempted—and most always are—to throw in one or two extra top priorities, they defeat the purpose of the thematic goal, which is to provide clarity around whatever is truly *most* important. This is best summarized by the wonderfully simple adage, "If everything is important, then nothing is." Something has to be *most* important.

Qualitative

The thematic goal is not a number, and it is not even specifically measurable. It is a general statement of a desired accomplishment. It requires a verb, because it rallies people to *do* something. *Improve, reduce, increase, grow, change, establish, eliminate, accelerate.*

Now, for those leaders who are disconcerted by the qualitative nature of all this, rest assured that a thematic goal will eventually be supported and clarified by metrics, numbers, and target dates. But this comes into play two stages later in the goal-setting process and should not happen sooner.

Time-Bound

The thematic goal does not live beyond a fixed time period, because that would suggest that it is an ongoing objective. To the contrary, it is a desired achievement that is particularly important during that period, and must therefore be accomplished in a corresponding time frame. That time frame is usually somewhere between three and twelve months, depending on the nature of an organization's business cycle and its unique situation.

For instance, a university often has a thematic goal with a relatively long time horizon, while a start-up company cannot usually afford to take such a long-term view. Some businesses have fixed costs and barriers to competitive entry that give their thematic goals a longer shelf life, while others can lose momentum or market share almost overnight and are forced to think in shorter increments.

Shared

The thematic goal applies to everyone on the leadership team, regardless of their area of expertise or interest. While it is true that some thematic goals will naturally fit largely within one particular executive's area of responsibility, it is critical that all team members take responsibility for the goal, and for doing anything they can to move the company—not just their own department—toward the accomplishment of that goal.

That means executives must remove their functional hats, the ones that say *finance* or *marketing* or *sales,* and replace them with generic ones that say *executive*. They must dare to make suggestions and ask questions about areas other than their own, even when they know relatively little about those areas.

And while that may seem to smack of a lack of trust among team members, it is actually a realization that the most insightful questions and ideas often come from people with a more objective—even naive—viewpoint than is possible for experts who are living and breathing an issue every day.

But a thematic goal, on its own, will leave an organization confused about what exactly to do. And that's where *defining objectives* come into play.

DEFINING OBJECTIVES

Once a thematic goal has been set, a leadership team must then give it actionable context so that members of the team know what must be done to accomplish the goal. These are called *defining objectives* because they are the components or building blocks that serve to clarify exactly what is meant by the thematic goal (see Figure 2).

Like the thematic goal, defining objectives are *qualitative* and *shared* across the entire team. And because they define the thematic goal, by definition they will be bound by time. It's worthwhile to examine the required elements of a defining objective in more detail.

Qualitative

Executives are often tempted to overquantify defining objectives because it gives them a sense of closure and cer-

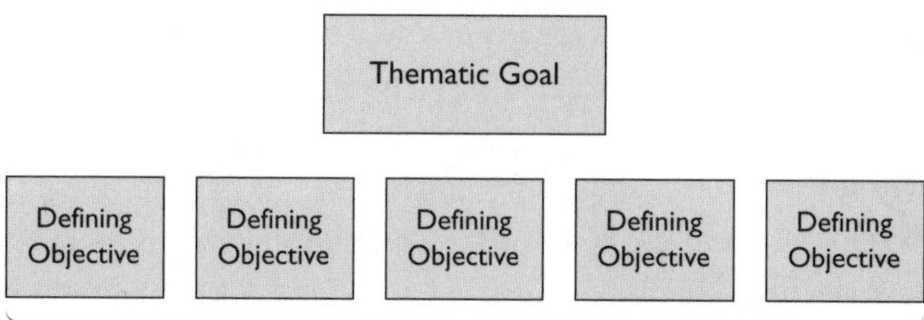

Figure 2. Goal Alignment Structure: Defining Objectives.

tainty, especially after struggling with the notion that the thematic goal was not quantified. However, assigning numbers and dates to defining objectives only serves to limit the involvement of leadership team members who cannot see how they might directly impact a numerical target. Rest assured, quantification comes into play soon enough.

Shared

Even though a defining objective seems to be geared specifically to the member of the leadership team with functional expertise in that area, it is critical that all leaders assume a very real sense of accountability and responsibility for achieving it. And even executives with little or no technical knowledge about that objective can and must play a critical role in ensuring that every angle is explored and every distraction is avoided. It is worth restating here: often the best suggestions and ideas about an issue come from people not closely involved in that issue. They bring valuable objectivity, even naïveté, to the table.

Time-Bound

When the thematic goal is no longer valid, the defining objectives also change.

STANDARD OPERATING OBJECTIVES

In addition to the objectives that provide definition around the thematic goal, it is critical to acknowledge the existence of other key objectives that a leadership team must focus on and monitor (see Figure 3). These are the ongoing objectives that don't go away from period to period. They vary from one company to the next depending on the industry.

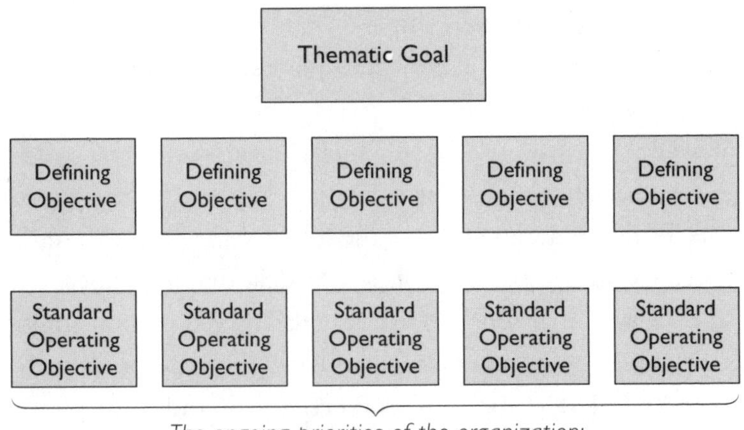

Figure 3. Goal Alignment Structure: Standard Operating Objectives.

Standard operating objectives often include topics like *revenue* and *expenses,* as well as other items like *customer satisfaction, productivity, market share, quality,* and the like. The danger for a company lies in mistaking one of these critical objectives, like revenue or expenses, for a rallying cry. Most employees find it difficult to rally around "making the numbers" or "managing expenses," knowing that these will continue to be trumpeted as critical over and over again in future periods.

But that's not to say that a thematic goal cannot involve one of these categories. If a company's biggest area of focus in a given period is accelerating revenue growth, then that could be the leadership team's thematic goal. Or maybe in the face of the loss of many key customers, the executive team decides that increasing customer satisfaction is the rallying cry for that period. Fine.

But leaders must resist the temptation to say, "Revenue is all that matters, because if we don't make our numbers, then everything else is immaterial." While that may be true in the most literal and extreme sense, it doesn't qualify as a thematic goal if it isn't unique to a given period. Instead, call it what it is: a critical but standard operating objective.

When leaders use these standard operating objectives as rallying cries, they create a "boy who cried wolf" syndrome, provoking cynicism and lethargy among employees who say, "Here we go again with the 'increase revenue' plea." Calling revenue a standard operating objective shouldn't diminish the importance of achieving it. In fact, it sends a message that the effort is always important, but not enough to generate success on its own.

METRICS

Okay, once the thematic goal, defining objectives, and standard operating objectives have been established, a leadership team can now start talking about measurement. But remember, without these other areas, metrics have little or no context. Even the most driven employees—including executives—will not be as motivated for hitting the numbers if they don't understand how they fit into the bigger picture.

Keep in mind that even metrics are not always quantifiable numbers. Often they are dates by which a given activity will be completed. Trying to artificially assign specific numbers to unmeasurable activities—which is a common mistake among many executive teams—is unwise because it encourages the achievement of arbitrary outcomes that may or may not contribute to the thematic goal.

For a free download of the model and other related tools, visit **www.tablegroup.com/silos**.

IDENTIFYING A THEMATIC GOAL

At first glance, deciding on a thematic goal can sometimes seem difficult. The key to finding the right one is to let a team discuss it for a while, without feeling the need to arrive at a quick decision. Oftentimes, a team's initial guess at a thematic goal will actually be one of the defining objectives that create the context for the goal.

For instance, consider a manufacturing company with a defective product that has caused harm to its customers. A child car seat, maybe. Or a bicycle. The first and obvious guess at a thematic goal might be "fix the product." However, a better answer might very well be "rebuild our credibility in the market." Certainly, one of the defining objectives will have to be "fix the product," but if that is all the company does over the course of the following six or nine months, it's still going to be in a world of hurt.

So be patient and constantly ask the question, "is this really the thematic goal, or is it merely one of many defining objectives?"

If you're still having a hard time identifying the thematic goal, you might be overthinking it. Often the thematic goal is deceptively simple. A consultant, who is not so close to the situation, or an employee deeper in the organization, who isn't so mired in overanalysis, might be the person to give you some perspective.

CASE STUDIES

This section provides fictional but realistic case studies from five different types of organizations to help you understand how the theory might apply in your organization.

Case Study #1:	*A worldwide pharmaceutical company*
Situation:	After two of its patents for best-selling drugs expired and generic competitors eroded its market share, a pharmaceutical company acquired a sizable, though slightly smaller, competitor in order to acquire a host of early stage drugs in the emerging anticholesterol market.
Thematic Goal:	Complete the merger of the organizations.
Defining Objectives:	Establish a comprehensive strategy for the new organization.

	Create a single, unified marketing message.
	Establish a single look-and-feel (logo, collateral, and so on).
	Eliminate redundant and underperforming products.
	Merge back-office systems and processes.
Time Frame:	Nine months.
Standard Operating Objectives:	Revenue.
	Market share by product category.
	Profitability by product.
	Employee turnover.
	Adherence to new product development and approval schedule.

Is the proposed thematic goal correct? Who knows? There is no definitive way to answer that question because it depends on what the leaders want to do with the business. This answer certainly seems reasonable, but then again, there could be other answers: acquire additional competitors, cut costs, and so on.

What is certain, however, is that there needs to be an answer of some kind so that executives—and employees up and down the organization—can get aligned and moving in the same general direction.

Only after a leadership team has established a thematic goal and defining objectives (and standard operating objectives) can it then start determining effective measurements. Most organizations I work with are good at measurements. However, assigning numbers to activities too early only distracts from the overall theme and gives people little context and incentive for achieving those numbers.

Case Study #2:	*A fast-food restaurant chain*
Situation:	Sales are slowly declining as more and more customers are starting to eat healthier food. Fast-food market share is shifting gradually toward alternatives like sandwiches and fresh Mexican food.
Thematic Goal:	Reposition the company for more health-conscious consumers.
Defining Objectives:	Revamp the menu offerings.
	Advertise the new offerings locally.
	Rebrand the company nationally.
	Redesign the restaurant facilities to fit the new market position.
	Teach employees to understand and promote the concept.

Time Frame:	Twelve months.
Standard Operating Objectives:	Maintain overall revenue and profitability.
	Maintain quality and consistency of food products.
	Pass all health inspections.
	Contain employee turnover.
	Continue safety and accident prevention.

Again, whether this is right or not depends on the specific situation, as well as on the judgment of the leaders.

Case Study #3:	***A two-year-old software company***
Situation:	Sales have increased faster than plan, along with the number of employees and customers.
Thematic Goal:	Establish an infrastructure for continued growth.
Defining Objectives:	Install a more scalable and comprehensive accounting system.
	Upgrade the customer tracking system.
	Establish policies and procedures for human resource management and hiring.

	Hire a chief administrative officer.
	Outsource IT support.
Time Frame:	Six months.
Standard Operating Objectives:	Make revenue numbers.
	Maintain cash flow.
	Retain key customers.
	Achieve positive assessments from market analysts.
	Get positive marketing/PR hits.

Once again, there is no way of knowing what the *right* thematic goal should be, though this one sounds reasonable. The key is to rally the entire leadership team—and thus, everyone else in the organization—around a single purpose for a given period of time, while simultaneously continuing to operate the company to plan.

Case Study #4:	***A church***
Situation:	Attendance at weekly services is up. Weekly receipts from the collection basket are growing. More and more people are joining the parish / congregation.
Thematic Goal:	Expand to meet demand.

Defining Objectives:	Add more Sunday services.
	Expand facilities.
	Offer more educational programs.
	Increase outreach.
	Grow the church staff.
Time Frame:	One year.
Standard Operating Measures:	Maintain attendance growth.
	Maintain collection receipts.
	Manage expenses.
	Increase number of people served through outreach.
	Achieve parishioner/member satisfaction targets.

These last two case studies highlight the fact that thematic goals are just as important during successful times as they are during a crisis. Not having a thematic goal when things are good only increases the likelihood that a crisis will eventually occur.

For instance, this church will begin to face dissatisfied parishioners and staff if it doesn't meet the growing demands that it is experiencing. Its leaders will look back and wonder how they could have failed to capitalize on such a great opportunity.

And in the previous case study, the software company will implode if it doesn't improve its infrastructure. This will lead to frustrated employees who will have to work twice as hard to do the work of running the company and satisfying customers—which will eventually lead to more and more dissatisfied customers, and a crisis.

Case Study #5: A university

Situation:	Enrollment is down slightly for the third consecutive year, test scores of entering students are slightly lower, and annual rankings have dropped compared to competing schools.
Thematic Goal:	Restore the school's reputation.
Defining Objectives:	Upgrade faculty in key disciplines.
	Launch new scholarship program for top students.
	Establish marketing program to key feeder schools in region.
	Hire PR firm.
	Revitalize alumni magazine and communications.
Time frame:	Eighteen months.
Standard Operating Objectives:	Maintain overall tuition revenue.
	Manage expenses.

Reduce number of students transferring out of the school.

Maintain percentage of graduating students who get jobs or are admitted to grad school.

Increase graduation rates.

Note that the time frame for this case study is longer than others because a university's calendar and culture often call for a more deliberate approach to implementation.

MANAGING AND ORGANIZING AROUND THE THEMATIC GOAL

Once a leadership team determines its thematic goal, defining objectives, and standard operating objectives, it needs to keep that information alive in the course of running the organization. And the place where it needs to be reviewed and discussed is during regular (usually weekly) staff meetings.

In another book, *Death by Meeting,* I recommended that there be no preset agenda at staff meetings, and that it be replaced by what I call a real-time agenda. Establishing a real-time agenda involves two steps, and the process should take no longer than ten minutes.

First, go around the table and give every member of the team thirty seconds to report on their three top priorities for the coming week. Even a team of twelve can do this in six minutes.

Then review your team scorecard, which is nothing more than a to-be-graded list of the items that make up the defining objectives and the standard operating objectives.

Let's take a look at the fast-food restaurant chain's scorecard in Figure 4.

Now, the colors assigned to each area are a simple, qualitative assessment based on the judgment of the leadership team members. As heretical as it may seem to allow executives to grade themselves without using hard numbers, the point of the exercise is to tap into the judgment

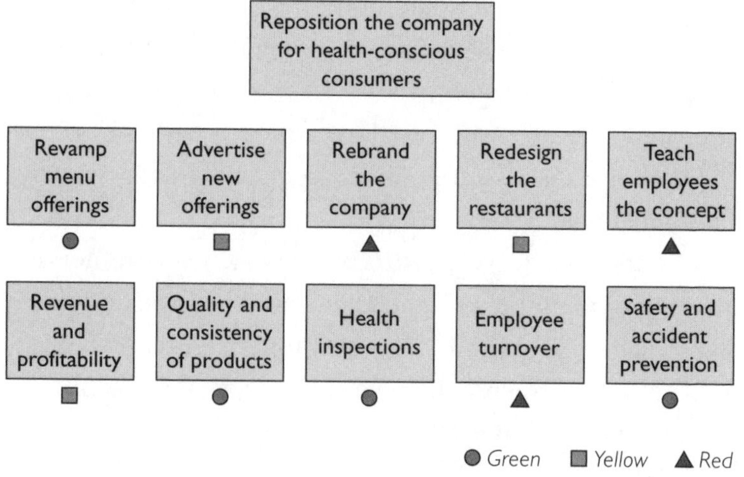

Figure 4. Sample—Weekly Scorecard for Fast Food Chain.

and intuition of the people running the company as to which areas are doing well and which aren't.

Rest assured, it will be next to impossible for the head of sales to say that revenue is a green if, in fact, it is not. That's because the CFO is going to say, "Wait a minute. I don't think I would call it green." And that's the point of the exercise, for the team to talk about each of the objectives and come to a general understanding of how they are doing against them.

The job of the leader is to quickly break ties by saying "Okay, let's call it orange" when people can't decide if something is yellow or red. Again, the purpose of the discussion is not precision but general assessment of performance. And it's not hard for most teams to agree on a rating.

Once the ratings have been done—and again, this usually takes five minutes—the team is ready to decide where to spend the time and energy available during the remainder of the meeting. And this would be the time for someone to challenge a teammate who is planning to spend a good chunk of time that week on an issue that is either disconnected from the thematic goal or related to an area that is already doing well. This kind of peer accountability about how team members are prioritizing their precious time and resources is key to an organization's ability to focus, and it is the thematic goal that provides the context for doing this.

Looking at the scorecard in Figure 4, it becomes clear that the agenda for the fast-food chain leadership team should have two primary topics of conversation: branding and employee development.

On the branding front, it seems that the branding effort is lagging behind advertising and restaurant redesign. Everyone—not just marketing—needs to feel responsible for asking about the situation, for getting clarity around what needs to happen to address it, and for assisting with the branding effort. Some might be able to contribute directly to the project, while others might simply offer up resources from their departments to help jump-start the project. Whatever the case, the key is that they recognize that none of them can succeed if they don't get this done.

However, this should not be mistaken for permission for individual team members to slack off or fail to deliver on commitments. While they must share responsibility for the thematic goal and pitch in to achieve it, they must also hold one another accountable over the long term for meeting standards of performance.

Employee development is the other issue that the fast-food executive team needs to discuss at the meeting because there are two problems in that area: too many people are leaving the company, and not enough of the ones who are staying are being taught how to represent the company's new direction. And this is certainly not HR's responsibility alone.

Everyone, from operations to marketing, needs to be involved in solving the retention and training problem, even if that means slowing the progress in one area (building out the new restaurants) to accelerate another (training the people who work there to understand the new value proposition).

If nothing else gets discussed during the meeting, these two areas (branding and employee development) must be. Needless time should not be wasted on discussions about the new menu or health and safety inspections.

As obvious as this may seem, it is an extremely common problem among many teams. All too often, executives spread their time evenly across all departments and issues, giving equal attention to every topic regardless of where it falls in terms of importance or progress. Meetings become show-and-tell sessions designed to give everyone time to talk about their departments and activities. This only reinforces silos and makes it more likely that critical issues get too little attention from the entire team.

Without the clarity of a scorecard that includes defining objectives and standard operating objectives, it is extremely difficult for them to avoid this. And without the existence of a thematic goal, it would all be impossible.

THEMATIC GOALS AND LONG-TERM CONTEXT

When a thematic goal runs its course and is largely accomplished, an organization must then come up with another, and then another. This raises the question, *Shouldn't all of this be part of a longer-term strategic direction?*

The answer is yes, but with some important caveats.

Too often, leaders of organizations choose one of two extremes when it comes to planning.

- They have no real long-range plan and make decisions reactively according to their short-term needs. Or . . .
- They have a detailed and analytically elegant three- or five-year strategic plan, which is designed to eventually roll up into a grand, all-consuming long-term goal.

And while I suppose it is better to have too much detail and information guiding decision making and prioritization rather than too little, it is nonetheless a problem that can lead to the same kind of flailing experienced by companies with no strategy at all.

Why? Because successful organizations achieve a delicate balance between predicting what is going to happen over the long term and responding to unexpected circumstances along the way. This calls for a planning approach that provides the right amount of context without unnecessary restrictions.

A thematic goal provides that context because it exists within the framework of six to twelve months, a time horizon that most businesses can accurately manage. Beyond that, organizations find that their plans become irrelevant or stale. Shorter-term goals, on the other hand, the kind measured in days or weeks, don't provide enough time for leaders and their employees to get their hands around something difficult.

Does that suggest the abandonment of weekly metrics? Absolutely not. But they should be established within the context of longer-term thematic goals.

And what about three- and five-year plans? They're fine too, as long as leaders don't artificially preserve them if they're no longer relevant—which is often the case in a dynamic market—and as long as they don't take the place of thematic goals.

As for BHAGs, every organization should probably have them. Like a core purpose, something else that Collins and

Porras describe in *Built to Last,* they can give leaders and employees a sense of why they get out of bed in the morning. But they don't provide enough guidance about what people should actually focus on once they get to work.

Consider that executives can be in solid agreement around a BHAG and still find themselves constantly working at cross-purposes. Take, for example, a community hospital whose BHAG is to be the best little community hospital in the world. Even if every leader of that hospital is completely committed to that BHAG, there is a great likelihood that silos will rise up within that hospital as executives with different responsibilities and interpretations of how that BHAG should be achieved lead their departments in different directions.

It's the thematic goal that ties it all together. Without it, the BHAGs lose connection to day-to-day activities, and weekly metrics become arbitrary and lifeless numbers that seem to serve no purpose other than their own.

A final thought about this. When a thematic goal is clearly established and communicated, employees should be able to look up from their work at any given time and see how they're contributing to an outcome that is far enough away to give them the ability to succeed, but not so far away that they cannot imagine ever being finished. They should be able to see how the company's long-term vision connects to its short-term objectives.

MAKING MATRIX ORGANIZATIONS WORK

Why matrix organizational structures became so popular I'm not really sure. There is certainly an element of flexibility and collaboration suggested by them, but in reality they are forums for confusion and conflict. They have certainly not contributed to the breakdown of silos; they've merely added an element of schizophrenia and cognitive dissonance for employees who are unlucky enough to report into two different silos.

But the matrix is here to stay, and so it is critical that we understand how to make thematic goals work within it. Happily, it turns out that a thematic goal is exactly what is needed to transform a matrix reporting structure from a tool of confusion to one of collaboration.

The real problem with matrices is that they put employees in difficult—maybe impossible—situations by asking them to please two different leaders who are not aligned with one another. By achieving clarity about the number one priority in an organization, and by clearly identifying the defining and standard operating objectives that contribute to it, companies will give their employees far less reason to fear being pulled apart at the seams.

And if an employee does start to feel some pull, it is a great opportunity for the leaders in charge to identify a crack in their alignment. Like a canary in a coal mine, a confused or conflicted employee can be a sign that the thematic goal and defining objectives aren't being communicated effectively, or more important, aren't being used to manage the organization from above.

GETTING STARTED

The first step a leadership team needs to take toward establishing a thematic goal and identifying its related components is to carve out enough time to discuss the organization's priorities. I can't imagine doing this effectively in less than two hours.

In some cases, a team will have to go back and clarify its overall purpose and strategy ahead of time in order to provide the context for identifying the thematic goal. So, as much as a full day might be advisable.

And for those who wince at the notion of spending yet another precious day sitting in a conference room while e-mail and other to-dos pile up back in the office, know this. Every executive team that I've ever taken through this exercise has come away with a very real sense of clarity and accomplishment. In most cases, it's as though the members have given themselves permission to stop paying attention to the noisy, extraneous distractions that plague them and focus on what truly matters.

Consider the time and energy that will be saved by providing your team with a unifying sense of purpose, by giving them an understanding of how everyone contributes to that purpose, and by making it easy to get employees throughout the organization rowing in the same direction.

Heck, that just might be worth *two* days. Good luck.

ACKNOWLEDGMENTS

I have more people than ever to thank for support and assistance. There is no way to name you all individually, because I would certainly leave someone off the list. But here's how I'm feeling.

First, I thank my wife, Laura, for your passion and authenticity, and for loving me and our children. And to those children, Conner, Matthew, Casey, and Michael, for your love and laughter.

I thank my parents, Rich and Maurine, and my brother, Vince, and sister, Ritamarie, for always being there for me. And to the rest of my extended family, Irish and Italian alike, and my in-laws, for forgiving me for not being around more.

Big thanks go to my colleagues at The Table Group, for making our company possible and for making it fun every day. Your contributions to this book, not to mention my life, are invaluable. And special thanks to you, Tracy. You are all over these pages.

To my many friends from St. Isidore church and school, and to my neighbors and childhood friends, thank you for teaching me how love extends beyond family. And to a few new friends and mentors in my life—Matthew Kelly, Tom Loarie, Pat Richie, Father Paulson Mundanmani, and Ken Blanchard—thanks for taking an interest in my development as a person. I cherish your friendship and counsel.

To my clients, thank you for allowing me to learn from you, and to occasionally help you and your organizations. And thanks to Susan Williams and Jim Levine, my editor and agent, for working so hard for me. And to everyone at Jossey-Bass/Wiley, for your commitment to me and The Table Group.

And of course, I thank the Lord, for everything I have and am, and for allowing me to enjoy my work. May it be pleasing to You.

ABOUT THE AUTHOR

Patrick Lencioni is founder and president of The Table Group, a firm dedicated to providing organizations with ideas, products, and services that improve organizational health, teamwork, and employee engagement. Lencioni's passion for organizations and teams is reflected in his writing, speaking, and consulting. He is the author of several best-selling books with over five million copies sold. When Lencioni is not writing, he consults to CEOs and their executive teams, helping them to become more cohesive within the context of their business strategy. The wide-spread appeal of Lencioni's leadership models have yielded a diverse base of clients, including a mix of Fortune 500 companies, professional sports organizations, the military, non-profits, universities, and churches. In addition, Lencioni speaks to thousands of leaders each year at world-class organizations and national conferences.

Patrick lives in the San Francisco Bay Area with his wife, Laura, and their four sons, Matthew, Connor, Casey, and Michael.

To learn more about Patrick and The Table Group, please visit www.tablegroup.com.

The Table Group is dedicated to helping organizations of all kinds function more effectively through better leadership, teamwork, and overall health.

Visit our website, and explore:

Consulting: Table Group Consultants provide practical, fast-paced consulting and training sessions to leaders and their teams.

Speaking: Patrick Lencioni brings his models on teamwork, leadership, and organizational health to tens of thousands of leaders each year.

Books: Patrick Lencioni's 11 best-selling books have sold over 5 million copies worldwide and tackle topics surrounding organizational health, leadership, and teams.

Products: *The Five Dysfunctions of a Team* and *The Truth About Employee Engagement* products were developed to help managers, leaders, and their teams address issues around teamwork and job fulfillment.

The Source for Organizational Health

www.tablegroup.com • 925.299.9700